Twayne's United States Authors Series

Sylvia E. Bowman, *Editor*

INDIANA UNIVERSTY

Claude McKay

TUSAS 271

Claude McKay

CLAUDE McKAY

By JAMES R. GILES
Northern Illinois University

TWAYNE PUBLISHERS
A DIVISION OF G. K. HALL & CO., BOSTON

Library of Congress Cataloging in Publication Data

Giles, James Richard, 1937-
  Claude McKay.

  (Twayne's United States authors series : TUSAS 271)
  Bibliography: p. 163 - 66.
  Includes index.
  1. McKay, Claude, 1890-1948.
PS3525.A24785Z68   818'.5'209   76-10154
ISBN 0-8057-7171-9

Dedicated to David Johnson,
what he was and is.

Contents

About the Author

James R. Giles, a graduate of Texas Christian. University and the University of Texas and an associate professor in the Department of English at Northern Illinois University, has published critical and scholarly articles on American literary naturalism and on American "minority literature." Essays on Frank Norris and Jack London have appeared in *Western American Literature* and *The Jack London Newsletter*, while articles on such Black writers as Charles Chesnutt, Zora Neale Hurston and Richard Wright have been published by *The Markham Review, Negro American Literature Forum*, and *Phylon*. Research in the private papers of the Negro naturalist, Willard Motley, has led to bibliographical and critical studies in *Resources for American Literary Study* and in *Studies in Black Literature*.

Literary admiration and personal friendship have recently led to extensive investigation of the fiction of the Chicano homosexual writer, John Rechy. In 1971, Rechy granted James and Wanda Giles an interview, which later appeared in *Chicago Review*. An article, which grew partially out of that interview, comparing Rechy's novel *City of Night* and James Baldwin's *Go Tell It on the Mountain* appeared in the November, 1974, special "homosexual imagination" issue of *College English*. The fiction of Joyce Carol Oates is another subject of interest; and Giles participated in an Oates seminar at the 1973 Modern Language Association convention.

A native of Texas, Giles has published essays about various aspects of the Texas experience in the Austin-based journal, *The Texas Observer*. The essays are about teaching the first Black literature course at North Texas State University, the nostalgia of country music, and the emotions felt on leaving Texas. Giles' fiction has appeared in *Descant, Riata*, and *Western Review;* and two stories have been anthologized in Dell paperback anthologies, *Innovative Fiction* and *No Signs from Heaven*.

Preface

Until recently, Claude McKay has been viewed primarily as a militant black poet who played an important role in the Harlem Renaissance and as the author who wrote three uneven novels which catered to the stereotype of the black man as an exotic primitive. Such evaluations are based upon a great deal of oversimplification, for McKay's relationship with the Harlem Renaissance was extremely complex. For instance, he never accepted many of the basic premises of such Renaissance spokesmen as Alain Locke and W. E. B. DuBois. His poetry is far from uniformly militant; in fact, he wrote a considerable body of lyric poetry unrelated to any idea of black revolt. But, most importantly, his fiction represents the major achievement of his career. Most critics of McKay would not accept this assertion of the importance of *Home to Harlem, Banjo,* and *Banana Bottom.* In fact, until Robert A. Bone's *The Negro Novel in America* (1958), no one had really treated the novels seriously. Nevertheless, the fiction develops a concept of black art that is based upon inspiration from the masses which was McKay's major contribution to Afro-American fiction.

Before dealing with McKay's poetry and fiction, it is necessary to clarify as much as possible his true relationships with "the Harlem Renaissance," with Marxist economic theory which tempted him during a significant part of his career, and with the Roman Catholic Church into which he was baptized late in his life. Also, the influence of Jamaica, the island of his birth, should not be ignored.

After devoting Chapter 1 to these biographical matters with supporting evidence from McKay's essays and his correspondence with Max Eastman, I treat the poetry and the novels separately. There is justification for such an approach, for McKay wrote his best poetry before turning to fiction in the late 1920s. Moreover, McKay, the poet, and McKay, the novelist, were quite different. In Chapter 2, I have dealt with only the most significant poems; I have omitted, for instance, any extended discussion of the apprentice work found in *Songs of Jamaica* (1912) and in *Constab Ballads* (1912). Chapter 4 treats McKay's one book of short stories, *Gingertown;* and a fifth deals with his two works of nonfiction — *A Long Way from Home* (1937) and *Harlem: Negro Metropolis.* The nonfiction is discussed last because it appeared last. Throughout this study, McKay's uncollected essays serve as supporting evidence for significant biographical and literary points. In addition to the two volumes of juvenile dialect poetry, the only body of McKay's writing excluded from discussion are his unpublished manuscripts. Clarence Major has recently published an article describing three of these manuscripts — "Romance in Marseilles," "Harlem Glory," and "My Green Hills of Jamaica." Major indicates that there are at present plans to publish only "My Green Hills of Jamaica," and that the three works are not of critical importance to this study. However, Major's discussion of their contents is summarized in Chapter 6, which is devoted to the last painful years of McKay's life and his several abortive literary projects. My central purpose in this study is twofold: I hope to demonstrate that Claude McKay was a major Harlem Renaissance poet — but not exactly in the manner in which he is commonly described — and that his greatest importance to Afro-American literature is represented by his three published novels.

Acknowledgments

I am grateful to the following for permission to make quotations from the works of which they hold the copyright: Carl Cowl and Hope McKay Virtue, representatives of the estate of Claude McKay, for quotations from *Banana Bottom, Home to Harlem, Gingertown,* "Boyhood in Jamaica," the "Author's Word" from *Harlem Shadows* and McKay's unpublished letters to Max Eastman; Harcourt, Brace and Jovanovich, Inc. for quotations from *A Long Way from Home, Banjo,* and *Harlem: Negro Metropolis;* Schocken Books, Inc. for quotations from *The Passion of Claude McKay,* edited by Wayne Cooper; Twayne Publishers, Inc. for quotations from *The Selected Poems of Claude McKay;* the editors of *Jewish Frontier* for quotations from "Lest We Forget;" the editors of *The Nation* for quotations from "Harlem Runs Wild;" Yale University Press for quotations from *The Negro Novel in America* by Robert A. Bone; Oxford University Press for quotations from *Harlem Renaissance* by Nathan Irvin Huggins; the Institute of Race Relations and the editors of *Race* for quotations from "A Black Briton Comes 'Home': Claude McKay in England" by Wayne Cooper and Robert C. Reinders.

I wish to express my personal gratitude to Carl Cowl and Hope McKay Virtue for their advice and encouragement during the writing of this book; to the staff of the Lilly Library of Rare Books, Indiana University, Bloomington, Indiana, for permission to make use of unpublished letters of Claude McKay and for assisting me in my study of the McKay-Eastman correspondence; to Clarence Major for taking the time to discuss with me his research into Claude McKay's unpublished manuscripts; to Northern Illinois University for financial support toward the completion of my work; to Sue Mellard for typing the final manuscript; and to Wanda H. Giles whose understanding of and enthusiasm for this study provided me with invaluable advice and assistance.

Chronology

1923 - 1933	Expatriate years in Europe and North Africa.
1925	Writes first novel, "Color Scheme," later destroyed.
1927	Alain Locke publishes *Four Negro Poets*, containing work by McKay.
1928	Publishes *Home to Harlem*, a popular success.
1929	*Banjo*.
1932	*Gingertown* and essay, "A Negro to his Critics."
1933	*Banana Bottom*.
1934	Returns to United States. Spends several months in welfare camp, Camp Greycourt, New York.
1935	Publishes the essay "Harlem Runs Wild."
1937	*A Long Way From Home*.
1938	Meets Ellen Tarry, Roman Catholic writer.
1939	Loses job with Federal Writers Project of the Works Progress Administration. Appears before subdivision of Dies Committee.
1940	Publishes *Harlem: Negro Metropolis* and the essay "Lest We Forget."
1943	Suffers stroke while working at a Federal shipbuilding yard. Moves to Chicago.
1944	October 11, baptized into Roman Catholic faith.
1945	Publishes essay, "On Becoming a Roman Catholic," and poem, "Look Within."
1946	In health resort in Albuquerque, New Mexico. Publishes poem, "The Middle Ages," and essay, "Why I Became a Catholic."
1948	Dies in Chicago; buried in New York after a service in Harlem.
1953	*Selected Poems of Claude McKay* published; essay, "Boyhood in Jamaica," published in *Phylon*.

CHAPTER 1

The Renaissance, Jamaica, the Party, and the Church

I The Renaissance

WHEN the following poem appeared in Max Eastman's magazine, *The Liberator* in 1919, Afro-American literature acquired a prophetic new voice:

> If We Must Die
> If we must die, let it not be like hogs
> Hunted and penned in an inglorious spot,
> While round us bark the mad and hungry dogs,
> Making their mock at our accursed lot.
> If we must die, O let us nobly die,
> So that our precious blood may not be shed
> In vain; then even the monsters we defy
> Shall be constrained to honor us though dead!
> O kinsmen! we must meet the common foe!
> Though far outnumbered let us show us brave,
> And for their thousand blows deal one deathblow!
> What though before us lies the open grave?
> Like men we'll face the murderous, cowardly pack,
> Pressed to the wall, dying, but fighting back![1]

As the writer of this poetry, Claude McKay, a Jamaican immigrant, suddenly found himself with a reputation as an important and promising young black poet. The brutal race riots throughout the nation in 1919 made it impossible to read phrases such as "mad and hungry dogs," "monsters," and "murderous, cowardly pack" as having any other reference than to white people; and that was certainly the way "If We Must Die" was read in 1919. For Afro-American literature, and most especially for black American poetry, this dic-

15

tion was indeed revolutionary. The assertion in the poem's second line that Negroes in America were besieged in completely surrounded, and thus completely vulnerable, ghettoes was to reappear in McKay's fiction as a major theme; and he was expressing an idea found frequently in the black American writing of the 1960s and early 1970s. However, the aspect of the poem that was most unsettling to the 1919 white view of the American Negro was its call for organized resistance to oppression. To Senator Henry Cabot Lodge, for instance, "If We Must Die" seemed a piece of demagogic heresy that demanded investigation.

In terms of the poem's strictly literary reception, "If We Must Die" was an almost unqualified success; and the timing of its publication could not have been better. Because of the promotion and encouragement of such Negro intellectuals as Alain Locke and W. E. B. DuBois and such whites as Carl Van Vechten, and because of a sudden plethora of black poetry and fiction of a dramatically higher quality than the work of earlier Negro writers, the 1920s produced the phenomenon of "the Harlem Renaissance." One of the most basic assumptions of this Renaissance was that it was time for a proud and independent black art to appear, and it is difficult to imagine a poem that would have better met this expectation than "If We Must Die." Inevitably then, McKay was seen as a leading figure in the awakening of black literature. Saunders Redding, in fact, describes him as inspiring the Harlem Renaissance.[2] *Harlem Shadows* (1922), McKay's first volume of poetry published in America, cemented his standing as a member of the 1920s black literary establishment; and any standard list today of the major writers of the Harlem Renaissance begins with Langston Hughes, Jean Toomer, Countee Cullen, and Claude McKay.

In the most meaningful sense, this evaluation is correct. To the degree that "renaissance" means simply a period of diverse and innovative art, McKay's importance and relevance are obvious. Philosophically, however, McKay often differed from other writers of the Harlem Renaissance. The awakening of Negro American art was supposed to come from within the racial group itself and was to be as free as possible of white control. McKay fitted the first half of this formula perhaps better than most people in 1919 realized; because of having worked at a series of menial jobs, he had deep associations and sympathies with the black masses. But, from the beginning, his career was guided and influenced by whites. Even in Jamaica, he had been discovered and promoted by Walter Jekyll, a

British aristocrat. In America, Frank Harris, the powerful editor of *Pearson's*, gave him his first opportunity to publish; and then Harris' rival, Max Eastman of *The Liberator*, continued to encourage him. McKay's association with Eastman was particularly, and often painfully, close until McKay's death; and in the very early 1920s Eastman made McKay an associate editor of *The Liberator*. The significance and irony of the fact that "If We Must Die" first appeared in a white magazine should not be ignored; for International Marxism waged in the 1930s a determined battle for control of Claude McKay's mind and art, and his final sanctuary was in the arms of the Roman Catholic church.

Perhaps even more important than his various relationships with white promoters was his attitude toward the black intellectual leadership — he never liked them, and he finally hated them. Animosity toward the black intelligentsia is strong in the McKay novels, *Home to Harlem* (1928) and *Banjo* (1929); and his animosity is usually voiced by Ray, the fictional representative of the author. In his autobiography, *A Long Way From Home* (1937), McKay makes it fully evident that Ray's attacks upon the Negro intellectual establishment reflect the novelist's own viewpoint. In his sociological and historical study, *Harlem: Negro Metropolis* (1940), the Jamaican's attack is so bitter and extreme that it seems almost paranoid. His feelings especially toward DuBois and Locke were complex. In the autobiography, he expresses much more admiration for DuBois' *The Souls of Black Folk* (1903) than for its author; for McKay considered DuBois cold and remote. When DuBois, the editor of *The Crisis*, denounced McKay's first novel, *Home to Harlem*, as a filthy and degenerate book, there was no longer any possibility of a close relationship between the two men. DuBois' attack initiated a long-standing misconception of *Home to Harlem* as a novel consciously and cynically imitative of Carl Van Vechten's *Nigger Heaven* that simplistically exploited the black man as an exotic primitive.

When Alain Locke edited a pamphlet entitled *Four Negro Poets* in 1927, he included poems by McKay, as well as by Langston Hughes, Jean Toomer, and Countee Cullen. His introduction emphasizes that this poetry represented the new militancy and artistic integrity of the Negro writer, but the author of "If We Must Die," who had already been given a prominent place in Locke's famous anthology *The New Negro* (1925), had been irritated by Locke's having arbitrarily retitled one of his poems. Again, no per-

sonal closeness ever existed between the two. In the three pages of
McKay's *A Long Way From Home* that are devoted to a discussion
of Locke, McKay stresses three points: As an individual, Locke was
autocratic and "high-handed"; his taste in the arts was severely
limited; and, most importantly, he was never the man to lead a black
literary renaissance.[3]

McKay's relationships with other writers of the Renaissance were
not always smooth. Countee Cullen, among the younger figures,
perhaps best represented the tone and spirit of the Renaissance. At
one point in the 1930s, McKay attempted to work with Cullen on a
new magazine of Negro art; but, in a June 28, 1933, letter to Eastman, he refers to Cullen with icy contempt.[4] Of all the figures in
either the older or the younger generation of 1920s black writers,
only James Weldon Johnson received McKay's unqualified
friendship and respect. The Jamaican admired Langston Hughes as
a poet; the two apparently never had any meaningful personal contact, but McKay's admiration for Hughes' art is, however, significant.

McKay's difficulties with men like DuBois, Locke, and Cullen
were partly the result of simple personality clashes. Also, until his
conversion to Catholicism, McKay had to rebel against all groups
and ideologies that tried to claim him; but he did have real
philosophical difference with the Renaissance establishment. In the
excellent study, *Harlem Renaissance*, Nathan Irvin Huggins in-
cisively assesses the "promotional" aspect of the movement: "A
positive self-image — there was cause for one — was considered the
best starting point for a better chance. Inequalities due to race might
best be removed when reasonable men saw that black men were
thinkers, strivers, doers, and were cultured, like themselves. Harlem
intellectuals, with their progressive assumptions, saw themselves as
the ones most likely to make this demonstration."[5] Anyone familiar
with DuBois' *The Souls of Black Folk* and its concept of "the
Talented Tenth" sees the point of Huggins' analysis. As eloquent as
DuBois' book is, its implications that racism can be rationally refuted
by Negro achievement now seem naive. An unmistakable assumption of this argument is that black writers should consciously but not
exclusively address enlightened white readers:

Since culture was not something that could be taken for granted, the announcement of its attainment by both white and black Americans seemed
natural enough. The vogue of the New Negro, then, had all of the character

of a public relations promotion. The Negro had to be "sold" to the public in terms they could understand. Not the least important target in the campaign was the Negro himself; he had to be convinced of his worth. It is important to understand this, because much of the art and letters that was the substance on which the New Negro was built and which made up the so-called Harlem Renaissance was serving this promotional end.[6]

This "promotional end" of the Harlem Renaissance, involving in part DuBois' famous theory that "the Talented Tenth" of the black and white races were morally obligated to "uplift" the masses, offended McKay. He did not feel that the masses needed "uplifting" by black or white intellectuals, and he did not attempt to end racism by appealing to reasonable white men. Indeed, what was revolutionary about the best of his black protest verse was its expression of the anger and hatred felt by the oppressed Negro. In it, he is concerned with the best means of reacting to racial injustice — that such injustice would not go away soon is assumed. In fact, a clear distinction between positive black and negative white values underlies his fiction; and the focus is upon the survival of blackness, and not upon either race's converting the other through rationality.

McKay disliked the idea that the Negro artist should "uplift" the masses, and he believed that the black common man was more in tune with his racial culture than were "the Talented Tenth." DuBois was outraged by *Home to Harlem* since it expressed these views. Its description of cabarets, rent parties, and lovely "brownskins" collectively forms a cultural image; and one of the book's central messages is the validity of this culture. DuBois' objection to the novel rested upon one challenge — how can the blacks progress if they are happy with the way of life described in *Home to Harlem*?

The answer is critical to an understanding of the subtlety and the complexity of McKay's best work. To a degree, his fiction and poetry express the primitivism common to literature about blacks in the 1920s. If primitivism were the major emphasis, the answer to the question of black progress would be simple — no progress was necessary. However, McKay's work is never that simple. In *Home to Harlem, Banjo,* and most clearly in *Banana Bottom,* one finds an early and incompletely formulated theory of black progress similar to that found in such contemporary black fiction as William Melvin Kelley's *A Different Drummer* (1962), Ronald L. Fair's *Many Thousand Gone* (1965) and Ernest J. Gaines' *The Autobiography of Miss Jane Pittman* (1971). Progress must come from within the black community, instead of being imposed from without. By maintaining his pride in his blackness and the heritage it implies, the black common man will determine his own progress. Always a believer in community solidarity, McKay advocated a "spontaneous," uncontrolled spiritual and economic rebirth for his people. Any control, even from the black intelligentsia, might dilute the African heritage in the name of a strictly Western concept of advancement.

In the article "A Negro to his Critics," which appeared in 1932, McKay discusses his conflict with the Negro intellectual establishment. He says that, even "If We Must Die" had made many of the black intelligentsia uneasy, ". . . to them a poem that voiced the deep-rooted instinct of self-preservation seemed merely a daring piece of impertinence."[7] On that basis, he asserts that ". . . respectable Negro opinion and criticism are not ready for artistic or other iconoclasm in Negroes. Between them they would emasculate the colored literary aspirant." (1). Still, "If We Must Die" had made his reputation in black America; and, while a portion of the Negro leadership had been disturbed by it and the rest of *Harlem Shadows*, that leadership did not thoroughly dismiss him until *Home to Harlem* appeared.

The article's main thesis is that McKay knows and admires the black masses and that the Harlem intelligentsia do not. His initial experiences in America had brought him into contact with Negro students. He expresses respect for the students, but he stresses that they do not truly represent "Aframerica":

But it was not until I was forced down among the rough body of the great serving class of Negroes that I got to know my Aframerica. I was perhaps then at the most impressionable adult age and the warm contact with my workmates, boys and girls, their spontaneous ways of acting and living for the moment, the physical and sensuous delights, the loose freedom in contrast to the definite peasant pattern by which I had been raised — all served to feed the riotous sentiments smoldering in me and cut me finally adrift from the fixed moorings my mind had been led to respect, but to which my heart had never held. (6)

This passage is crucial to an understanding of McKay. Critics have overgeneralized in regard to the association in his fiction of blackness with *total* spontaneity and "instinct"; but a central theme of *Home to Harlem, Banjo,* and *Banana Bottom* is that Negroes are still capable of unstructured emotional behavior, especially when it is appropriate. Not only is that capacity a positive thing in the three novels, it is what enables the Afro-American to resist dehumanization by the white power structure. McKay does not equate spontaneity with passivity or inability to think, as some critics seem to imply. But Jake of *Home to Harlem* and Banjo, his two prototypes of the Negro masses, are able to make unqualified and unashamed response to immediate "physical and sensuous delights." Jake and Banjo find these "delights" in cabarets, rent parties, and brothels.

The nostalgic overtones of this passage are, in themselves, interesting. Ray, the character who links *Home to Harlem* and *Banjo*, is obviously patterned after his creator. Originally from Haiti with a university background, he struggles throughout the two novels to live the kind of free, unstructured existence that Jake and Banjo enjoy. But Ray's education and his childhood training are persistent handicaps to that kind of commitment. Finally, at the end of *Banjo*, he decides that it is possible to wed "instinct" and "intellect"; and he vows to "vagabond" around the world with Banjo. This ending is aesthetically weak and philosophically unconvincing; for, as will be shown, McKay always had trouble dealing with Ray. Still, the novel obviously relates to the essay, "A Negro to his Critics." After the publication of *Banjo*, McKay continued to desire a free, unstructured life *which did not negate his intellect*. In fact, in 1933, the year after the appearance of "A Negro to his Critics," he published *Banana Bottom*, his best artistic statement of the ideal wedding of instinct with intellect. Its main character, Bita Plant, makes a believable commitment to such an ideal.

Bita personifies McKay's only successful artistic statement of another aspect of his theory about black progress. Intellectually, he wished to be unrestricted by race or any other consideration; and he believed that there were important things to be gained from the Western heritage. He did not feel it necessary to cut himself off from the great artistic and philosophical traditions of Europe and America. Tolstoy, D. H. Lawrence, and Hemingway constituted a legacy he could not, and would not, repudiate. James Baldwin's famous statement of cultural alienation is relevant here: "the most illiterate among them [whites] is related, in a way that I am not, to Dante, Shakespeare, Michelangelo, Aeschylus, Da Vinci, Rembrandt, and Racine. . . ."[8] Throughout his life and writing, McKay struggled to believe that such separation from the best in white Western culture was not necessary for the black man.

Educated in British-controlled Jamaica, he was trained to believe that culture and art were essentially what England and Europe declared them to be. His life was a never-ending struggle to over-come such a limited definition; and he was an early spokesman for the validity of African culture. Still, his belief that the great ideas of the West transcended racial concerns would always have kept him from adopting a position of total *cultural* separatism.

McKay's position was ultimately a very complex and idealistic one. He deeply believed in the importance of African culture, black folkways, and solidarity within the black community. He also felt that the great intellectual legacy of the West should not be repudiated by black Americans. However, he distrusted the leadership of any intellectual elite — black or white — because such an elite would inevitably seek to control; and he believed that the Negro intelligentsia were hopelessly ignorant and, thus disapproving, of black folkways.

McKay did not, therefore, intend for his art to serve a "promotional" or evangelical mission in the Harlem Renaissance sense of "uplifting" the masses. His fiction is primarily a realistic description of a valid way of life. Ironically, however, it is also the most complete and detailed investigation of a concept of positive blackness produced in Afro-American fiction during his lifetime. Unlike his poetry, his novels make extensive use of technical innova-tion for the purpose of truly black expression. Even though his per-sonal associations were almost exclusively with white editors and promoters and though his fiction was rejected by much of the 1920s Negro establishment, he wrote three of the most intensely black novels yet published in America. It is a comment upon the limitations of the Renaissance movement rather than upon McKay's work that his poetry, which was always hampered by conscious im-itation of traditional British models, was infinitely more acceptable to the contemporary Negro cultural establishment than his fiction.

Because of McKay's attitudes and the technical innovations in his fiction, his admiration of Langston Hughes is not surprising. By utilizing the techniques of blues and jazz, Hughes produced a poetry more faithful in some ways than McKay's to black life; and his crea-tion of Jesse B. Semple also implies his rejection of the "uplift" thesis. Jesse, like Jake and Banjo, is presented as requiring no salva-tion either from reasonable whites or from intellectual blacks. McKay and Hughes overcame the philosophical limitations of the Renaissance in their creation of a distinctly black literature.

When McKay wrote "A Negro to his Critics," he was living in Morocco, North Africa; and his African experience from 1930 to

1934 is part of another complexity in his relationship to the Renaissance proper since he was absent from America during most of it. He had spent the last part of 1919 and most of 1920 in England, where he first read Karl Marx. For an extended period, Marxism held a strong attraction for McKay; but, by the mid-1930s, he had become a strident and vocal anti-Communist and denied that he had ever accepted Marxism. After returning to New York from England in late 1920, McKay left for Russia around the middle of 1922 and spent approximately one year there. Fifteen years later, he still referred to this year as "the magic pilgrimage." When he left the Soviet Union in 1923, he did not return to America; for, from 1923 until late 1930, he explored Europe — France, Germany, Spain. Although he was on the fringes of the American expatriate movement in Paris for part of that time, he never really felt a part of the "lost generation" because he knew that the main cause of his chosen exile was racism and not the same sort of philosophical, personal, and economic factors which had motivated Ernest Hemingway, Gertrude Stein, and their group. Still, McKay was *physically* closer to the "lost generation" than to the Harlem Renaissance for most of the 1920s.

McKay's letters to Eastman make it clear that, when he did return to the United States, the Harlem Renaissance was over. The Depression had destroyed America's interest in black writing, as it had much else that was both good and bad about the 1920s. The black America he came back to was that of Richard Wright's Bigger Thomas in *Native Son*, and not Jake's or Banjo's; and McKay personally encountered this reality almost immediately upon his return. In September, 1934, he had to work as a laborer in a welfare camp; and, although the pay was a dollar a day, fifty cents was deducted for "maintenance." Besides his physical and spiritual degradations, McKay found an even greater disadvantage in his camp existence: "The *big* drawback is that I see no chance of creative work. And a life like this should be endurable only if you can be compensated by creative work."[9] Early in 1935, he escaped the camp; but it left its marks on him. Because he knew that he had contributed significantly to the revival of black letters, he had difficulty in accepting the artistic and personal degradation of the welfare camp. One feels that McKay was attempting to comprehend his status as a black American writer in virtually all the Eastman correspondence of this period.

In effect, McKay was asking one question as to whether or not he had been forgotten by black and white America — especially by black America — despite the fame he had achieved in the Afro-American community with "If We Must Die" (even if it had made some people uneasy) and with the financial success he had had with *Home to Harlem* (even if the Renaissance establishment repudiated it). In large part, the answer was painfully in the affirmative, for the Depression did to McKay's literary prospects what it did to those of more than one writer, black and white. More basically, however, the Depression undercut the whole black arts movement because in the 1930s, black America was in no position to reward any artist. It was a desperate time for Richard Wright and Langston Hughes, as well as for Claude McKay.

The Negro intelligentsia which in the first place had largely disliked *Home to Harlem* must have felt that, at a time when black people were unemployed and hungry in greater numbers than ever before, a writer who emphasized cabarets and lovely, erotic "brownskins" was irrelevant. Although such a view implies a vast oversimplification of McKay's fiction, such short-sighted criticism — caused by the critics' desire for literature that had "social relevance" — temporarily damaged or delayed the reputations of more than one important writer during the 1930s. The case of F. Scott Fitzgerald immediately comes to mind; and, on at least one level, there is a parallel between McKay and Fitzgerald. Both acquired reputations based on the dramatic and spectacular elements in their fiction rather than upon the serious concerns underlying their novels. In a period of shifting critical values, they inevitably suffered.

To a large degree *Home to Harlem*'s popularity with white readers had been based on the fad in the 1920s of reading about the exotic (and erotic) Negro. The Depression left few people with the time or money to cultivate fads. Also in the 1930s the white critical establishment wanted the suffering of fictional victims of economic injustice to be dramatically and starkly obvious. It was a time for the Joads of John Steinbeck's *Grapes of Wrath* and not for Jake and Banjo. Throughout this period, McKay expressed to Eastman a hope that he would again be successful and recognized as a writer; for he could not accept how radically the world had changed.

During most of the period in which "the Harlem Renaissance" was a viable and cohesive movement, McKay was in Europe, Russia, or North Africa. When he returned, it had been killed by the failure of the white establishment's economic system. There is an irony implicit here which might have served as the basis for more than one novel. It would have been interesting to read about Jake's life during the Depression, but McKay's career as a publishing novelist ended in 1933 with *Banana Bottom*. The Depression's effects upon the black artist and, more importantly, upon the Negro common man offered dramatic and tragic proof of the main ideas in all three McKay novels and especially in *Banjo*. The white capitalistic system is portrayed as corrupt and cruel in McKay's fiction, and the Jamaican was fully aware of its power over nonwhite people. When the system disintegrated, largely because of its own selfish excesses, McKay should have felt that his Old Testament prophecy had been vindicated. That the American black man suffered the most because of the excesses of whites should not have surprised him. Thus, a novel about Jake in the Depression years would have allowed McKay to carry the implications of *Home to Harlem* to their logical conclusion; but his own problems during those years ended his career as a novelist. While he continued to write fiction, he was never able to publish another novel after *Banana Bottom*.

Taking into consideration McKay's lifelong associations with white sponsors, his personal and philosophical differences with Negro intellectuals such as DuBois and Locke, and his absence from the United States during most of the 1920s, one hesitates to say that McKay really was an integral part of the movement which "If We Must Die" had partially inspired. Yet, he was clearly a major force in the new black writing which resulted in the maturity of Afro-American literature; for he instinctively rejected in his novels the articles of faith that limited much Negro writing of the Renaissance, and he anticipated the kind of black fiction that would come years later. While his poetry was conservative in form, it was, to use Melvin B. Tolson's phrase, "radical" in content.[10]

II   *Boyhood in Jamaica*

It should be emphasized, however, that McKay's importance in literary history is not limited to his contributions to the Harlem Renaissance or to Afro-American literature; for, since he was a native of Jamaica, he has to be viewed in relationship to West Indian writing. Kenneth Ramchand stresses McKay's importance as a pioneer in the development of West Indian fiction: "The themes of McKay's fiction, the critical issues it raises, and the overall pattern of his *oeuvre* make him the type of the West Indian novelist."[11]

Besides *Banana Bottom*, Jamaica is relevant to other McKay writing. Jamaica is the setting of four of the stories in *Gingertown*;

and nostalgia for the island of childhood innocence is a major theme in his poetry. Moreover, his first two books are devoted to Jamaican dialect verse. Yet, his relationship to that native island was as complex as most things about McKay. His autobiography, for instance, virtually omits discussion of the years prior to his arrival in New York City; and the immediate impression one gets from this omission is that the Jamaican background, as well as everything else that happened prior to McKay's entrance into New York literary circles, was unimportant. However, when one realizes that *A Long Way From Home* must not be read as a traditional autobiography, this impression vanishes. As will be discussed, *A Long Way From Home* is really two things: an account of McKay's inner struggle with all the forces that attempted to seduce him away from black consciousness, and the statement of a black aesthetic theory. The book focuses, therefore, only upon that part of the author's life in which he was indirectly arriving at a commitment to black art by struggling with other, temporary, loyalties.

The novelist's letters to Eastman reveal mixed feelings about Jamaica. Particularly in the early 1930s just before his return to the United States from Morocco, McKay felt an urge to visit the island of his birth; however, he consistently balances this feeling with expressions of the impossibility of going home permanently. The West Indies were simply too remote from the centers of Western cultural activity for a man intent upon a literary comeback. The critical and popular failure of *Banana Bottom* seems to have destroyed its author's urge to go home even for a visit. He then felt that it was more than ever necessary to be in New York if he was ever going to regain his former popularity. Sadly, McKay seems to have accepted the verdict that *Banana Bottom* was an artistic failure; for, in his correspondence with Eastman, he mentions the novel in a negative context: "Whether poetry or prose, my writing is always most striking and true when it is a little reminiscent and nostalgic. The vividness of 'Home to Harlem' was due to my being removed just the right distance from the scene. Doing 'Banjo' I was too close to it. 'Banana Bottom' was a lazy dream, the images being blurred from long distance photography."[12] As will be seen, *Banana Bottom* is much more than "a lazy dream"; but it is significant that McKay dismissed it as that, while simultaneously expressing the desire to produce another *Home to Harlem*. Obviously, only New York could inspire the kind of book he felt it necessary to write. So Jamaica was dismissed both in a real and in a literary sense.

Later however, McKay again focused his literary attention upon
that West Indian island. In 1953, *Phylon* published an extract from
an "autobiography of brown childhood" entitled *East Indian, West
Indian* which McKay had been writing with Cedric Dover. The fragment of that autobiography that was published posthumously in
Phylon is entitled "Boyhood in Jamaica," and it reveals much about
the forces which molded McKay's thought. Undoubtedly, the most
interesting aspect of "Boyhood in Jamaica" is that, despite the suffering and the ideological changes McKay experienced during the
last fourteen years of his life, its main ideas are perfectly in keeping
with those found in *Banana Bottom*. Jamaica is remembered as an
idyllic place, despite its poverty; its beauty is described in both
natural and human terms; and the opening paragraphs emphasize
the natural harmony of McKay's childhood home. Although the
Jamaican was fascinated by the iron and steel grandeur of New York
City, his fascination obviously did not negate a response to the rural
simplicity of the West Indies. Even more important, however, is his
stress upon Jamaica as a land of harmonious human relationships in
which different races lived together in relative peace: "In spite of its
poverty, Jamaica was like a beautiful garden in its human
relationships."[13]

In this posthumous essay, McKay is aware of his African heritage.
He talks about the popular worship of Obeah, a West African god, in
his village; and it might be mentioned that one of *Banana Bottom*'s
major conflicts is between Obeah and Christ. After describing a
childhood custom of making "moonshine babies" out of pieces of
broken crockery, McKay adds: "I am not sure, but I think father told
us that the making of these moonshine babies was an old African
custom and that different villages used to compete in the making of
them" (136). His father is remembered as ". . . a wonderful teller of
African stories . . . and African customs" (141); and this passage calls
to mind a chapter in *Banjo* in which the main characters exchange
folk tales. The fact that McKay consciously grew up with a strong
African heritage is relevant to his years in Morocco and to the black
consciousness found in most of his writing.

An awareness of Africa as the mother continent is vitally important to McKay's Jamaican fiction; and perhaps the best scene in
Banana Bottom describes the terror induced in Priscilla Craig, a sexually frustrated white missionary, by the sight of some African tribal
masks. Priscilla and her husband, Malcolm Craig, personify an in-
tolerant, perverted Christianity which attempts to destroy black

spontaneity and happiness. Despite McKay's late conversion to Catholicism, one cannot read *Banana Bottom*, or *Banjo* for that matter, without feeling that his attack is directed at Christianity as a force that works with white imperialism against black natives — and the roots of that animosity toward Christianity can be found in "Boyhood in Jamaica."

In "Boyhood in Jamaica," which also deals with the subject of British imperialism, McKay's tone in his discussion of the English is surprising in view of the animosity which had resulted from his 1920 visit. As will be seen more fully in Chapter 5, the 1920 experience was only the beginning of a series of events which made McKay feel that the British Empire was as sinister a force as any in the world. Indeed, his memories of his Jamaican childhood so mellow his attitude toward the English, that even Rudyard Kipling would have enjoyed McKay's tribute to cricket as a promoter of racial brotherhood: "I do know that the game of cricket helped to draw tighter 'the bonds of Empire' and helped coloured and whites to understand each other better" (136). The most interesting comment about the British accompanies a tribute to the humanitarianism of the colonial governor of Jamaica during the novelist's childhood: "in the British Empire, for all its wickedness, there have always been men of exceptionally high principles" (140). This statement is one of the very few instances in McKay's mature writing where the emphasis is not upon British "wickedness."

In "Boyhood in Jamaica," McKay sees nothing positive about the United States. The country where he earned his greatest fame and where he spent the last fourteen years of his life after leaving North Africa is treated with intense bitterness. As he remembers, the United States introduced him to racism; for anti-Semitism had also been unheard of in Jamaica: "I never heard the word 'Christ-killer' until I came to America" (143). McKay concludes his comments on America by restating one of the central themes of the novels and of much of the poetry which he had produced between 1919 and 1933:

And that is the main danger of Americanization. The carriers are prejudiced and materialistic. Most Americans, it seems to me, from the extreme left to the far right, believe that what the rest of the world needs is more sanitation and material luxury: enamel bathtubs, gleaming wash basins, and two bottles of milk for every person. They don't realize that millions in other countries don't like and won't drink milk as American adults do. Or that there are millions of Moslems and Hindus who insist that water for washing must be poured onto the body, as has been done from the most ancient times (143).

When this view is extended to include all white imperialistic nations (with the United States treated simply as the most powerful one), it is the central one of all three of McKay's novels. Although he attempted to find convincing, positive answers to the problem created by such materialism in the novels, he really succeeds only in *Banana Bottom*.

"Boyhood in Jamaica" ends on an assertive note, but it does so when McKay turns his attention specifically to Jamaica and then to universal black progress. He regards his island home as inspiring a new era of black pride: "Indeed, as I have said, the people of Jamaica were like an exotic garden planted by God. And today I see them as something more. I see them as a rising people, and sometimes I think that the Negroes amongst them will give leadership to the Negroes of the world in the great struggle that lies ahead" (143). The essay's last paragraph completes his thought:

> For the creeping pressure of disease tells me that this is my last book, and I will never again see my green hills and the people I loved so much.
> It is the farewell testimony of a man who was bitter because he loved, who was both right and wrong because he hated the things that destroyed love, who tried to give back to others a little of what he had got from them and the continuous adventure of being a black man in a white society. Happily, as I move on, I see that adventure changing for those who will come after me. For this is the century of the coloured world.[14]

These two passages parallel the ending of McKay's autobiography, *A Long Way From Home* (1937), which was the last important statement published during his lifetime of positive black pride. The concluding emphasis in both works supports the thesis that black consciousness was always the major theme in McKay's writing. It was his treatment of the black experience in a white world that assured his literary importance.

What this posthumous essay of 1953 *seems* to add is the concept of Jamaica as the example of a new world order. Ray of *Home to Harlem* and *Banjo* is from Haiti, and he expresses no great expectations concerning that island. The other West Indian characters in *Banjo* primarily discuss European imperialism. As mentioned, one would hardly know from *A Long Way From Home* that McKay was from Jamaica. The island of his birth is treated nostalgically in most of the poetry, but nostalgia by definition can have little to do with revolutionary change or expectations. However, the concept of Jamaica as the catalyst of a more humane world is not so unprecedented in McKay's writing as it appears to be. Bita Plant of *Banana Bottom* is the only character in the three novels who develops a satisfactory sense of identity; and her identity, based on her final commitment to Jamaican peasant life, can only be achieved after she rejects white religion. Although the novel does not editorialize, one can assume that Bita's decision represents the triumph of black pride over the temptations of white materialism, religion, and prestige. Bita does not want "enamel bathtubs" or "gleaming wash basins"; she desires only pride in herself and in her people. When seen as the conclusion of McKay's fictional treatment of the black struggle to maintain identity in a white world, Bita's decision has relevance beyond her own characterization.

"Boyhood in Jamaica" is evidence then that the island played a significant role in the development of McKay's thought. He never returned there after his departure for the United States; he seems to have never seriously considered a permanent return; but, as he remembered it toward the end of his life, his home gave him a vision of a world without crippling racism. Moreover, his outlook inevitably differed from that of a Negro writer born in the United States. For example, Richard Wright's Mississippi childhood left him with a world view that was permanently clouded by a grim pessimism; but Ralph Ellison's experience can be compared to McKay's, for, to Ellison, the "frontier environment" of Oklahoma induced in him a belief in life's possibilities which childhood in the Deep South or in an urban ghetto could never have given him. At any rate, the Jamaican years may help explain McKay's emphasis upon the necessity to enjoy life despite the problems resulting from discrimination. If so, the absence of any significant discussion of those early years in McKay's autobiographical *A Long Way From Home* is all the more frustrating since "Boyhood in Jamaica" demonstrates McKay's desire to correct this situation. We know, in fact, that McKay once intended to complete his description of his Jamaican childhood. Clarence Major tells us that the unpublished "My Green Hills of Jamaica" is a fragmentary and poorly written manuscript about McKay's growing up in his native island. McKay conceived with Cedric Dover, author of *Half Caste* (1937), the plan for a joint autobiography to be entitled *East Indian, West Indian*. However, "aside from the fact that Dover and McKay did not share literary, social or political views, the project never got off the ground."[15]

McKay's hopeful tone in "Boyhood in Jamaica" is surprising in view of the rejection and bitterness of the last year of his life when the essay was presumably written. Of more importance, however, is the contrast between the overall optimism and nostalgia of the posthumous essay and the bitter negativism of McKay's best poetry. "Boyhood in Jamaica" helps clarify a significant point concerning the author of "If We Must Die," for his contrast of Jamaica, the future home of black pride, to America, the land of racial oppression, is crucial to an understanding of the nature of hatred in McKay's work. Hatred is quite different from hopelessness; but, during the period of his most important work (1919 - 1937), his voice was the most intensely angry one in Afro-American literature — but that emotion did not produce a sense of hopelessness. There is, for instance, a dramatic difference between his writing and much of Richard Wright's; for Wright's personal and racial alienation gave to his *Uncle Tom's Children* and *The Outsider* a pessimistic view that often approaches hopelessness. Although McKay's Jake and Banjo are never hopeless, they, as several critics have suggested, are not comparable in terms of their acceptance of racism to Mark Twain's Jim in *Huckleberry Finn.*

Although black American writers have nearly always been motivated *to an extent* by emotions such as anger and hatred, part of Claude McKay's historic importance is that he stated such feelings more openly than any previous black novelist or poet. Moreover, despite such anger and hate, especially prominent in his novels, McKay assumed that positive answers could be found for the problem of Negro suffering; and this fact may be a clue to the relative artistic success of the three novels. *Home to Harlem's* focus is initially upon the joys of Harlem life; and anger enters with an abruptness that is harmful to the book's balance. *Banjo* is by far the most angry of the three novels and the picture it presents of the Negro's position in a white imperialistic world is so bleak that its "happy ending" is not aesthetically plausible. *Banana Bottom,* however, represents a beautiful balance between anger and racial optimism.

In a personal note in the last paragraph of "Boyhood in Jamaica," McKay analyzes himself as "a man who was bitter because he loved, who was both right and wrong because he hated the things that destroyed love"; and this analysis may help to explain why his career went so steadily downhill after 1933. It is evident from the Eastman correspondence that McKay's personal suffering shook his faith in ultimate racial justice during most of the last fourteen years of his life. He was bitter between 1934 and 1948 — bitter toward Negro intellectuals; toward the Communist Party and the white leftists who had once courted him; bitter toward the United States as a nation which seemed determined to deny racial justice; in effect, bitter toward the world. When he published *Harlem: Negro Metropolis* in 1940, that bitterness had virtually become paranoiac.

The ideas that his bitterness resulted from love and that he was both "right and wrong because he hated the things that destroyed love" are significant in themselves. McKay wanted a world that provided room for Jake, Banjo, and Bita Plant to live and develop as they should. Simply stated, he wanted a humane world; but the years between 1934 and 1948 were the years of Hitler, Mussolini, Stalin, and the Martin Dies Committee. If McKay meant the word "love" to imply decency and tolerance, he had much to be bitter about since extermination camps, pogroms, and character assassinations were the international reality of the last fifteen years of his life. He was certainly "right" to hate the forces that shaped that kind of reality, but it is interesting to speculate upon the manner in which he had been "wrong." He may have meant that his hatred had become so all-consuming that it weakened his own capacity for objectivity and fairness. Such an admission would be particularly relevant to *Harlem: Negro Metropolis*. Or McKay might have meant that the horror, both international and personal, of those years had almost caused him to lose any faith in ultimate human justice and decency. If so, the optimistic passages found in "Boyhood in Jamaica" verify that the loss was never complete and that, during the peak of his career, his vision of Jamaica as a "garden" of human brotherhood kept his anger and hatred from turning to despair. During the last fifteen years of his life, poverty, neglect, and disease did make this vision difficult to maintain. Indeed, McKay's letters to Eastman indicate that personal suffering and disillusionment concerning fundamental human decency had much to do with his acceptance of the Catholic Church as a substitute for black consciousness.

III   *The Party and the Church*

Prior to analysis of McKay works, McKay's commitments to Marxism and Catholicism should be considered. Although his introduction in London to Marxist theory and his journey to Russia are discussed more fully in relation to *A Long Way From Home*, since the two events are vital to the peculiar structure and theme of that book, the basic nature and degree of the Jamaican's commitment to Marxist thought should first be considered. The nature of McKay's interest in and break with Communism is best illustrated in a 1944 letter to Max Eastman:

> For although I was once sympathetic to their cause, I was never a Communist. I had a romantic hope that Communism would usher in a classless society and make human beings happier. All I saw in Russia was that Communism was using one class to destroy the other and making people more miserable, which was quite contrary to what my idea of Communism was. And I don't think that it is merely Stalin turning things wrong in Russia. I think the concept of a fractricidal [sic] class war is contrary to the ideal of humanity. Besides, Communism is quite a primitive ideal and I don't see how modern society could go back to it.[16]

The Eastman correspondence also reveals a significant shift in McKay's feelings about the Communist movement in the late 1930s. Beginning around 1925, he became increasingly angry at the Moscow government and Marxist literary critics. He had reservations from the beginning about the degree of honesty in the Party's rhetoric concerning racial brotherhood, and he always resented pressures to write Marxist propaganda, rather than literature. Because of Wayne Cooper's excellent collection of McKay's short fiction, nonfiction, letters, and poetry in *The Passion of Claude McKay*, we now know that the Jamaican did address the Third Communist International during his "magic pilgrimage" to Russia. McKay's speech contains three especially interesting comments: he speaks of having been pressured into becoming a spokesman for "Negro radicalism in America to the detriment of my political temperament"; he comments bitterly upon "the great element of [racial] prejudice among the Socialists and Communists of America," and ends his speech with the "hope" that blacks will soon be in the front ranks of "the Red Army and Navy of Russia" in its battle against "the international bourgeoisie."[17] As Marxist criticism of McKay's novels became more hostile and it became evident to him that racism was not limited to the Communists of America, he lost his faith in Moscow's potential leadership in the battle for the rights of his race. Such disillusionment is certainly understandable and, in fact, farsighted. After 1938, however, McKay expresses again and again in his letters to Eastman the belief that he is being persecuted by "Stalinists." He senses their hostile presence in the upper echelons of President Franklin Delano Roosevelt's administration, in the Works Projects Administration from which McKay was expelled in 1939, in the publishing business, in short, everywhere. McKay's insistence in 1944 that he "was never a Communist" and that Communism is an unworkable, "primitive ideal" probably resulted from his intellectual differences with the Party and from his sense of being personally threatened by it.

In a literal sense, the statement that he "was never a Communist" is true. He refused, even in Russia, to join the Party; his reasons for this refusal are discussed in Chapter 5. However, as Chapter 5 also shows, one cannot read the Russian section of *A Long Way From Home* and the letters in the 1920s to Eastman without feeling certain that McKay's initial attraction to Marxism was considerably stronger than the 1944 letter quoted above would lead one to believe. The most revealing aspect of that letter is the comment that he had once had a "romantic hope" about the future of Communism, and nowhere is his "romantic hope" better illustrated than in his 1921 *Liberator* article "How Black Sees Green and Red."

The article opens with an account of McKay's experiences in Trafalgar Square while selling copies of the *Workers' Dreadnought*, Sylvia Pankhurst's London-based Marxist journal. After this introduction, "How Black Sees Green and Red" focuses upon the England-Ireland conflict and upon the reasons for McKay's complete sympathy with the Irish revolutionaries. Ireland, he says, is the only white nation that is exploited by Western imperialism in the same way that most of the nonwhite areas of the world are. For him, then, the animosity between Negroes and Irish-Americans in the United States lessened in importance. He believed that the Irishman and the American Negro were engaged in an identical international struggle and that it was imperative for both to realize that fact. Indeed, the surge of emotion that McKay felt for the Irish nationalists leads him into an expression of faith in the universal proletariat; and his faith is so strong that he dismisses the racist prejudices of white workers as unimportant.[18] One should assume that this early devotion to the proletarian cause was deep, sincere, and "romantic"; within less than ten years, the white worker's prejudice against blacks mattered a great deal to McKay.

Two passages from "How Black Sees Green and Red" that specifically concern the Irish revolution reveal the limited nature of Claude McKay's concept of Marxism:

I suffer with the Irish. I think I understand the Irish. My belonging to a subject race entitles me to some understanding of them. And then I was born and reared a peasant; the peasant's passion for the soil possesses me, and it is one of the strongest passions in the Irish revolution.

The English proletarian strikes one as being more matter-of-fact. He likes his factories and cities of convenient make-shifts. . . . And when he talks of controlling and operating the works for the workers, there burns no poetry in his eyes, no passion in his voice. . . . That is a further reason why England cannot understand the Irish revolution. For my part I love to think of communism liberating millions of city folk to go back to the land.[19]

Stephen H. Bronz correctly analyzes McKay's early understanding of Communism as having been rooted in ". . . racial equality and a return to the soil." He had not really seen Marxist doctrine in relation to the reform of industrialism.[20] This view is puzzling since McKay's fiction and poetry both reveal a strong response to the peculiar excitement and energy of industrial society; but the Jamaican influence may be of significance in this reaction. In "Boyhood in Jamaica," McKay's stress upon the beauty and peace of West Indian communal life may help explain his initial view of Marxism as especially applicable to racial justice and agrarianism. McKay's 1921 description of himself as a "peasant" by birth and upbringing — one possessed by "the peasant's passion for the soil" — is highly reminiscent of the mood and language of the posthumous autobiographical fragment. It is peculiar, but true, that this peasant identity explains both McKay's appreciation of English Romantic poetry and his initial devotion to Marxism. Such a limited vision of a highly complex social and economic theory was "romantic," and it inevitably foreshadowed disillusionment.

Although *A Long Way From Home* ignores the fact that McKay's break with *The Liberator* resulted from his focusing while assistant editor and ultimately coeditor upon racial, rather than universal, concerns, McKay was determined that the number of *Liberator* articles concerned with matters of race be proportional to the percentage of blacks in the United States population. Always a more realistic Marxist, Eastman feared that such an editorial philosophy would offend white workers who read *The Liberator*. Thus, while McKay was strongly committed to a limited definition of international socialism in the early 1920s, the limitations of that definition caused problems from the beginning. The most important thing to say, therefore, about McKay's involvement with proletarian thought is that it never seriously tempted him to renounce his strong black consciousness. Nonetheless, Marxism had by far the strongest influence upon him of any nonblack doctrine until his conversion to Catholicism.

As mentioned, the Eastman correspondence indicates that McKay's religious conversion resulted from a diminution of faith in ultimate justice for Negroes in particular and for human beings in general. On June 1, 1944, McKay wrote a letter describing the attraction which Catholicism was then beginning to have for him; and one remark is particularly important: "From the social angle I am quite clear and determined: I know that the Catholic Church is the one great organization which can check the Communists and probably lick them."[21] That same month, in the letter which denies any previous commitment to Communism, McKay gave Eastman a more detailed account of his growing interest in the Church. In this letter, he closes on a particularly bitter note: ". . . I have lost my idealism, for I don't think the world is interested in ideals any more, excepting the lies of liberals."[22] It is easy to see how such disillusionment might have led McKay to search for justice in another, completely spiritual, world.

Characteristically, McKay justifies his interest in Catholicism in two ways. That the common man has always been religious is his first argument, and this contention leads him to attack intellectuals and Communists: "I would hazard that about 95 per cent of humanity believes in God. And that belief among ordinary mortals, workers and peasants, is greater than among the upper strata. Yet, it seems to me that the more the intellectual *knows* of life, the greater its mystery. . . ."[23] The Church had come to have some of the same appeal for McKay that Communism had once held. In 1921, the religion of Karl Marx seemed the best hope for the "peasant"; twenty-three years later, however, McKay saw Marxism as a destructive rival of the Church; but his identification with the "peasant" class is still intact.

His second justification concerns his belief in God, and it is less plausible. When he tells Eastman in 1944 that he "was always religious," as a sympathetic reading of his poems would prove,[24] his statement is extremely difficult to accept, as will be shown in the next chapter.

It is significant, however, that McKay does not try to argue for a religious reading of his novels; for in them he consistently treats Christianity as a force in league with imperialism. Later, in a published article entitled "On Becoming a Roman Catholic," he did assert that his anger about religion was always directed against Protestantism alone;[25] but one cannot accept that explanation. In the 1940s, McKay adopted a revisionist approach toward his religious past more than once; but he could not dismiss the fact that he had been an articulate freethinker during his youth in Jamaica, where he had been given an early push toward intellectual rationalism by the influence of his brother. In the 1944 letter to Eastman, he does not try to deny his past as a "freethinker," but he does repudiate it:

As a free-thinker I had read glowing accounts of the beauty and glory of the Pagan world, which was smashed by Christianity. But human life (I discovered) under Paganism was horrible and hopeless indeed, with the Emperors even setting up their horses as Gods. And everywhere, people in their misery was hoping [sic] for a savior, a Spirit who would be greater than the Ruler-Gods. And so when Jesus came the Western world was ready and ripe for his Gospel.

I can see more clearly now just why he came to the poor and downtrodden. And in spite of all that I have read to the contrary, I do believe that the ancient and medieval world had a wonderful asset, which we lack today, when a Pope of Rome, with the authority of Jesus, could say to a stubborn ruler: Stop! For what you do is contrary to the Will of God! Stop or you will be excommunicated! . . . I have always felt that if ever I became religious I would join the Catholic Religion, as I would only need to accept without thinking matters of pure faith.[26]

One cannot help but compare the phrase, "if ever I became religious," to the earlier assertion in the same letter that he had always been religious. More interesting, however, is the passage concerning the Pope. McKay desperately wanted to believe that, sometime in world history at least, a force capable of controlling dictators had existed; for such control was obviously lacking in the 1940s. Also, it is hard to imagine a more total rejection of free thought than his anticipation of being able to "accept without thinking." McKay was exhausted; he had been disappointed, emotionally and intellectually, by men too often. More than once, Eastman begged his former protege not to join the Church. It is at least an interesting footnote in the history of American radicalism that the one-time editor of *The Liberator* bases his appeal on the idea that McKay's religious conversion would compromise his philosophical battles with doctrinaire Communists.

Later, when McKay had been baptized, he attempted to minimize the philosophical debate with Eastman: "After all, Max, what is

Truth? It seems to me that to have a religion is very much like falling
in love with a woman. You love her for her color and the music and
rhythm of her — for her Beauty, which cannot be defined. There is
no reason to it, there may be other women more gorgeously
beautiful, but you love One and rejoice in her companionship."[27]
This description is more in keeping with the patterns of McKay's life
than is the rationalization found in the earlier letter. One is not surprised that the author of *Home to Harlem* and *Banana Bottom* made
an emotional commitment in response to his love of a "Beauty" that
is fittingly personified as a sensuous woman. Still, one has the feeling
that McKay is simply tired of dealing with abstract philosophical and
political ideas — "After all, Max, what is Truth?"

In 1945, the novelist published an account of his turn to
Catholicism in "On Becoming a Roman Catholic." The essay contains all of the least appealing aspects of his letters to Eastman, and
there is no stress on the mysterious "Beauty" of the Church. He
gives 1938 as the date that he "began thinking seriously about the
Catholic Faith,"[28] and he then briefly outlines his life. Even in this
autobiographical sketch, he thoroughly repudiates his previous
achievement as a writer — he had been a "pagan," and his novels
and early poems are marred by this impiety. Still, he attempts the
argument that, even in his pagan period, he had always been
"religious-minded" (43). However, his impulse toward belief had
been overshadowed by the social upheaval of the time and by the
prevailing concepts of art:

I visited Russia soon after the Revolution. It was a shock to find there a
government and a society basically anti-human nature. It rested upon the
theory that the working-class could not better itself and take power, except
by civil war with wholesale slaughtering of other workers and the middle
and upper classes. So I left them alone and moved on to sample the rest of
Europe. I swung around from place to place in the circle of disillusioned
liberals and radicals. I forgot about social revolution, instead I wrote risque
stories and novels. At that time that was the fashion in writing (43).

McKay's depression and disillusionment at the time of this article
are obvious. His fiction is infinitely more than some "risque stories
and novels," and one finds it incredible that he dismisses his
products as being merely that. The critics who had attacked *Home to
Harlem* in 1928 as "filth" must, however, have been overjoyed by
"On Becoming a Roman Catholic" — particularly by the implica-

tion that his novels had been written only because such fiction was fashionable and lucrative. Indeed, he might as well have pleaded guilty to capitalizing upon the popularity of Van Vechten's *Nigger Heaven* as DuBois had charged. One would regret the self-denigration of "On Becoming a Roman Catholic" if McKay had simply been a mediocre writer, but the importance of his writing to Afro-American and West Indian literary history makes it doubly painful.

Spain was the catalyst for McKay's fascination with Catholicism; when visiting that country, he had felt that "Spaniards of all classes" respected ". . . the dignity of the individual and the oneness of all humanity" (43). To McKay, Protestantism, not Christianity, was the source of evil; and, since this belief was his personal one, it is unarguable. The attack in his fiction is, nevertheless, upon Christianity; he makes no distinction in the novels between positive Catholicism and negative Protestantism.

The remainder of "On Becoming a Roman Catholic" is an attack upon Communists and "left wing Liberals," and two particular passages reveal more than McKay perhaps intended. The first one describes his friendship with Ellen Tarry, ". . . the only Catholic intellectual among Harlem's hectic melange of pagans and Protestants" (45), who offered him friendship, he says, at a time of intense personal pain. Since the Marxist critics were viciously attacking *A Long Way From Home* and since he was appreciative of "any group opposing the Communists" (45), Ellen Tarry's generosity began to represent Catholic benevolence to McKay; and he contrasted that generosity with the indifference and neglect of most of his former leftist associates. Thus, one feels that a unique combination of personal gratitude and resentment had much to do with his choice of a last philosophical home.

In the context of Claude McKay's entire career, his final commitment to Catholicism diminishes in importance — and so does his earlier stormy flirtation with the Communist Party; for his role as a spokesman for black pride in prose and poetry transcends all aspects of his personal life. During the years between 1919 and 1937, he produced three novels which constitute a major fictional achievement in Afro-American and in West Indian literature; a volume of short stories which approaches the theme of racial identity from a variety of directions; the first significant militant Negro poetry to be published in America; and *A Long Way From Home*, which fails as autobiography, but not on other, equally meaningful levels. While it must be said that his poetry is not always overtly concerned with racial matters (he wrote some surprisingly good love poems, for instance), he insists in *A Long Way From Home* that his racial identity underlies all his writing.

CHAPTER 2

The Poetry: Form versus Content

I N his autobiography *A Long Way From Home*, McKay describes
the reception of "If We Must Die" among the black masses:
". . . for it the Negro people unanimously hailed me as a poet. Indeed,
that one grand outburst is their sole standard of appraising my
poetry. It was the only poem I ever read to the members of my
[railroad] crew."[1] McKay was not exaggerating, for the poem immediately established McKay as a leading figure in the Harlem
Renaissance; and it, along with the novel *Home to Harlem*, were the
two single works for which McKay was best known throughout his
lifetime. While *Home to Harlem* dismayed many blacks, especially
such a major promoter of the Renaissance as DuBois, "If We Must
Die," even if it caused some nervousness, was generally accepted by
Negro intellectuals and the masses alike. Ironically, *Home to
Harlem* undoubtedly owed much of its success to its exotic and sen-
sational appeal to white readers (it was a best-seller); but, when it is
read today, its integrity as a distinctly black book is obvious. Because
of a highly traditional form and diction, "If We Must Die" may
easily be read as not directly applicable to black issues; in fact,
Winston Churchill made the poem relevant to the Allied cause when
he read it publicly during World War II. In a March 23, 1939, letter
to Max Eastman, McKay tells about a Jewish friend's reading the
poem and proclaiming that it must have been written about the
European Jews persecuted by Hitler: "I replied I was happy he was
moved by the universal appeal. . . ."[2] After the war, McKay asserted
that he had never considered "If We Must Die" as a specifically
black poem and also that he had never regarded himself as a black
poet.[3] Yet, in *A Long Way From Home*, he formulates a literary
theory based upon a concept of the inseparability of his art and his
race. Certainly Nathan Irvin Huggins is correct when he argues that,
when "If We Must Die" first appeared, ". . . no one could doubt

that the author was a black man and the 'we' of the poem black people too."[4]

There is more irony in the fact that "If We Must Die" carries the weight of McKay's poetic reputation. Its militant and direct call to arms is not typical of his other protest poems; and a great deal of his poetry cannot be classified, directly or indirectly, as black protest. *The Selected Poems of Claude McKay* includes nostalgic lyrics about Jamaica, songs celebrating nature and love, and a few poems concerned with the suffering of the working classes. There are also poems which reflect themes found in nineteenth-century English Romantic poetry. In addition, as Huggins correctly emphasizes, the tone of much McKay poetry is marked by a stoicism similar to that found in the writing of such English Victorians as Rudyard Kipling, William Ernest Henley, and A. E. Housman;[5] and such Victorian stoicism can hardly be said to complement any plea for a militant uprising. Conflict between McKay's passionate resentment of racist oppression and his Victorianism in form and diction creates a unique kind of tension in many of his poems, which weakens their ultimate success.

More importantly perhaps, "If We Must Die" is not his best poem. Time has proved that it can be quite effective as propaganda for a number of causes; but, viewed aesthetically, it has obvious flaws. The traditional, stilted diction that so often marred McKay's work is particularly evident in this poem: "Making their mock at our accursed lot," "So that our precious blood may not be shed in vain," "O kinsmen! we must meet the common foe!" The juxtaposition of this highly derivative language with the use of epithets such as "hogs," "monsters," "murderous, cowardly pack," etc., is especially jarring. There are certain poems, stories, and novels which, because of the time and circumstances of their appearance, transcend strictly literary judgment; and "If We Must Die" is one of them — for its positive influence upon the growth of black pride should never be ignored. The fact that critics recognize it as the inspiration for the Harlem Renaissance assures its permanent importance.

The poem's propaganda value was unwittingly emphasized by *Time* magazine in its coverage of the prison rebellion in Attica, New York, in 1971. *Time* printed on September 27, 1971, the first stanza of "If We Must Die" with the explanation: the prisoners, described as "self-styled revolutionaries," ". . . passed around clandestine writings of their own; among them was a poem written by an unknown prisoner, crude but touching in its would-be heroic style." In a letter to the magazine, published on October 18, 1971, Gwendolyn Brooks called attention to its blunder: the "unknown" poem, she wrote, was "a portion of one of the most famous poems ever written — known to Hitler, elementary school children, to say nothing of Winston Churchill." This incident is in keeping with the bitter struggle of Claude McKay's life because, a quarter of a century after his death, he was apparently unknown by a white establishment journal but was defended by a black writer of the stature of Gwendolyn Brooks. What would have most pleased McKay about the incident would have been the recognition of his work by the black prisoners of Attica. Yet there is the level on which the poem must be judged simply as poetry; and, on this level, it is not a complete success.

One example of a better McKay poem is certainly "The Harlem Dancer":

> Applauding youths laughed with young prostitutes
> And watched her perfect, half-clothed body sway;
> Her voice was like the sound of blended flutes
> Blown by black players upon a picnic day.
> She sang and danced on gracefully and calm,
> The light gauze hanging loose about her form;
> To me she seemed a proudly-swaying palm
> Grown lovelier for passing through a storm.
> Upon her swarthy neck black shiny curls
> Luxuriant fell; and tossing coins in praise,
> The wine-flushed, bold-eyed boys, and even the girls,
> Devoured her shape with eager, passionate gaze;
> But looking at her falsely-smiling face,
> I knew her self was not in that strange place.[6]

The unmistakable black protest in this poem about oppression is made subordinate to the individual tragedy of this one woman. The language does not slip into the stilted diction that one finds in "If We Must Die," as well as much of McKay's other poetry; and the two central metaphors are controlled and intrinsically black in nature. The woman's voice is compared to the music produced by black flutists; and the analogy of her body and a "proudly-swaying palm" has tropical overtones which call to mind McKay's West Indian origins. There is a finely understated irony implicit in these two metaphors: "a picnic day" connotes a happy, relaxed celebration, and the woman's body suggests pride.

The dancer, however, is victimized and dehumanized both because she is black and because she is a woman. Her job is no "picnic" to her, but it has not destroyed her pride. The phrase "swarthy neck" demonstrates a stylistic device that one finds in many McKay poems, for he was a master of the trick of reverse connotation: "swarthy," when seen in the context of the dancer's pride and dignity, is not a negative term. Finally, the concluding couplet effectively reinforces the poem's central idea: the dancer does have dignity and pride, but they can be retained only if she removes herself mentally from the reality of her existence.

"Harlem Dancer" is a black poem that can be read as a protest against the oppression of the Negro. However, it can also be related to the dehumanizing of women or, for that matter, of everyone in modern society. But its impact is made possible by the graphic picture of this one dancer's suffering. While "If We Must Die" is abstract and generalized, "Harlem Dancer" is personal and immediate. Because of this difference, the first poem is more effective propaganda; the second is better poetry.

"Harlem Dancer" is, however, no more typical of McKay's poetic accomplishment than "If We Must Die." Diversity of subject matter, as well as considerable variation of aesthetic merit, makes it difficult to generalize about his poetry. Reliance upon quite traditional forms and diction is perhaps the one characteristic that is applicable to most of McKay's poems; for he never approached an innovative, intrinsically black style in his verse. His novels, while influenced by such white writers as D. H. Lawrence, Ernest Hemingway, Sherwood Anderson, and James Joyce, reveal at least an interest in experimenting with black form and language. The extreme traditionalism of his poetry, in contrast to his fiction, is not really surprising, since McKay's Jamaican education and reading had been based firmly upon the major British poets. From the point quite early in his life when he began to think of himself as a poet, his models were such major English writers as William Shakespeare, John Milton, William Wordsworth. He thus was committed from the beginning to the poetry which he had initially been taught to admire. In *A Long Way From Home*, he does express his admiration for the classical black poet, Antar; but, in the passage in which he asserts the black integrity of his own art, he refers to Lord Byron, John Keats, and Percy Bysshe Shelley.

Since McKay had apparently never considered writing fiction until it was suggested to him by Frank Harris after his arrival in

America, he had no initial allegiance to any traditional concept of the novel. As a result, he was receptive to the influences of contemporary white prose innovators and was willing to experiment with inherently black form and language. Obviously, a pioneer work like *Home to Harlem* is far from being free of white influences, but it certainly reveals more of an attempt to merge language and form with a concept of blackness than does a poem like "If We Must Die." For its experimental, innovative form and diction alone, McKay's fiction is as important, if not more important, than his poetry in the history of Afro-American literature. This evaluation seems correct despite the emphasis by most McKay critics upon the poetry, and despite the power of the defiance of the best protest poems.

Only at the beginning of his career did McKay depart from traditional poetic form and diction. His first two books, *Songs of Jamaica* (1912) and *Constab Ballads* (1912), are devoted to Jamaican dialect verse. Even here, however, there is a British influence; for McKay consciously thought of himself during this apprentice period as the "Jamaican Bobby Burns." After the two books of dialect verse, McKay published two other volumes of poetry, *Spring in New Hampshire* (1920) and *Harlem Shadows* (1922). *Harlem Shadows*, which contained "If We Must Die" and most of his best protest poetry, was the volume which cemented his position as a leader of the Harlem Renaissance. Alain Locke, especially, regarded it as a prime example of the "new Black consciousness" of the 1920s; and, as has been observed earlier, Locke celebrated McKay, as well as others, in *Four Negro Poets*, as the leading voices of the black awakening.

McKay's "Author's Word" in *Harlem Shadows* is revealing, for he feels compelled to explain the conservative nature of his poetic style. Emphasizing the heavily British character of his early education and his reading, he states that he instinctively expresses his "most lawless and revolutionary passions and moods" in a language and form based on those "older traditions" which are "adequate."[7] Obviously, he had accepted the idea that the British masters represented poetry in its highest manifestation. This "Author's Word" is important because it is one of the rare occasions in which McKay comes to grips with the central paradox of his poetry — its often revolutionary content is expressed in extremely traditional form and diction.

Because McKay revised his poetry all his life, it is best to study his individual poems as they appear in the posthumously published

Selected Poems of Claude McKay. Virtually everything of any merit in *Spring in New Hampshire* and in *Harlem Shadows* is found in this collection, along with a good deal more. *Selected Poems* is divided into five sections: "Songs for Jamaica," "Baptism," "Americana," "Different Places," and "Amoroso"; but "Baptism" and "Americana" contain most of the work upon which his poetic reputation must finally rest.

I *"Baptism" and "Americana"*

"Baptism" and "Americana" contain the black protest verse for which McKay is best known, as well as his proletarian poems, and poetic expressions of urban malaise and of spiritual struggle. Two poems, "The White House" and "The White City," are important discussions of the hatred produced by racism. "The White House" might have been subjected to several levels of interpretation that McKay did not intend if he had not discussed it specifically in *A Long Way From Home.* The necessity of explaining the poem arose because Alain Locke included it in *The New Negro* and changed its title to "White Houses." This change bothered McKay because the new "title was misleading. It changed the whole symbolic intent and meaning of the poem, making it appear as if the burning ambition of the black malcontent was to enter white houses in general. I said that there were many white folks' houses I would not choose to enter."[8] Locke's justification for the title change is interesting — he told McKay that he feared that the poem would be thought to refer to the official home of the President of the United States and cause McKay trouble when he attempted to return to America. Although McKay replied that such a limited reading of "The White House" would be "ridiculous,"[9] he later related exactly what he had in mind when he wrote the poem: "My title was symbolic, not meaning specifically the private homes of white people, but more the vast modern edifice of American Industry from which Negroes were effectively barred as a group."[10]

This interpretation does seem the most logical and meaningful. At any rate, the real subject of "The White House" is the hate produced in black people excluded from participation in the rewards of American industry and capital.[11] An interesting distinction is made between "anger" and "hate," for the opening lines of the sonnet graphically depict the alienation forced upon blacks by American society; in fact, a theme of dehumanization emerges that is comparable to Ellison's concept of invisibility. The result is "anger," but this "anger" will be borne "proudly and unbent." In the concluding couplet, McKay stresses the necessity of not allowing this proud and justified rage to be transformed into "hate": "Oh, I must keep my heart inviolate/Against the potent poison of your hate."

Moreover, McKay also pleads for the "wisdom" and "the superhuman power" to obey "the letter" of the white society's law (78). McKay is arguing that the twenty-four-hour-a-day reality of discrimination inevitably produces an abiding bitterness in the black mind; yet, for the sake of physical safety, that outrage must be masked by obedience of the legal and extra-legal "laws" of "The White House." More importantly, the poem warns that one must guard against letting that justifiable "anger" become a pervasive, self-consuming "hate"; for McKay would have agreed with Baldwin that unrelieved hatred most destroys the one who hates. Perhaps he also implies that, even while obeying the oppressive rules and customs of the white society, the black individual must in his heart reject their brutal "spirit." An inward integrity can be maintained even in the face of unavoidable oppression.

"The White House" represents a quite different attitude than that of "If We Must Die"; however, the two poems are not really inconsistent — the 1919 sonnet's call for decisive action is relevant only to extreme emergencies, matters of literal life and death; but "The White House" focuses upon every day discrimination and oppression. "The White House" also makes effective use of the McKay device of reverse connotation: "The pavement slabs burn loose beneath my feet,/A chafing savage, down the decent street" (78). Both "savage" and "decent" convey an effective irony. In the eyes of the powerful white structure which excludes him, the black man is a "savage"; seen as a lesser being, he is viewed as unworthy to take part in American capital and industry.

Yet, the poem emphatically makes the point that the corruption rests within the "white house," not in those excluded from it. The truly evil savagery is at the basis of the white establishment, but the result of that evil is a "savage anger" in the excluded. The irony intensifies the theme of the dehumanization that is inevitably produced in those people who live in a society in which they are prevented from legitimately competing but are simultaneously condemned for not succeeding. Morally, the "white house" is indecent; but its sheer weight and power overturn any humane definition of morality. In the American capitalistic structure, decency is judged solely on the basis of who possesses the symbols of material prosperity. One of McKay's best poems, "The White House" still seems unnaturally restricted by its sonnet form.

Black hatred is also the subject of "The White City," but its mood differs from that of "The White House." The idea of exclusion from the white establishment is again dominant: the city is seen "through a mist," the port is "fortressed," and the black speaker's relationship to the white society is an illegitimate one that is comparable to that of a "wanton" lover's. However, the attitude toward the hate produced by such exclusion represents a significant departure; the speaker, far from wishing to be kept "inviolate" from that "dark Passion," regards it as the single factor that most sustains his identity. One phrase in particular, "I muse my life-long hate," can be taken as a description of the inspiration behind a poem like "The White City"; it grew out of McKay's bitterness toward the race that oppressed him.

Such an interpretation is relevant to much black literature — often the positive fact of its creation rests upon essentially negative emotions. McKay's special kind of irony lies behind the idea that the intensity of the speaker's hatred produces a "heaven in the white man's hell." Intensity of emotion, even if a negative one, offers a salvation from the "white city's" attempt to make him into "a skeleton, a shell"; for, at this point in his career, passionate realization of self was probably the nearest McKay came to any acceptance of a heaven concept. "The White House" and "The White City" neatly balance each other; the first poem is an idealistic expression of the desire not to be consumed by a crippling hatred, but the second represents a realistic awareness that an oppressed individual must feel some degree of hate for his oppressors. If he does not, he really ceases to exist.

The power and injustice personified by the United States is the immediate subject of the sonnet, "America." Hate-producing discrimination is a theme in it, but two other concepts are equally important. The attraction McKay felt toward the energy and power of his adopted country mingles with his anger at being excluded from its inner workings, and the conflict produces the stoicism in McKay that the critic Nathan Irvin Huggins has discussed and that the poem expresses:

> Although she feeds me bread of bitterness,
> And sinks into my throat her tiger's tooth,

> Stealing my breath of life, I will confess
> I love this cultured hell that tests my youth! (59)

A note of Victorianism is present in the idea of a "test" that results in the attainment of real manhood; such a concept is in keeping with the philosophy of a Kipling, for instance. Traditional stoicism also keeps the poem's diction from achieving true freshness and maximum force. In the poem, the last four lines move away from the strictly personal and, in an omniscient voice, prophesy the eventual doom of racist America: McKay's message seems clear — a society founded on hate and injustice will ultimately be destroyed by its own corruption. The flux of ideas in the sonnet is interesting — McKay begins with an expression of mingled attraction and bitterness that one feels is intensely personal, and he ends with a godlike proclamation of the inevitable defeat of the fortress of injustice. Obviously, despite the fact that he spent a large part of his adult life in the United States, McKay could never find his identity satisfactorily in a society that so excluded his race.

Black protest is the overt subject of two remaining sonnets, "The Lynching" and "To the White Fiends." The first half of "The Lynching" is marred by a self-conscious view of the victim as a Christ figure; but, when McKay turns his attention to the lynchers, he achieves real horror:

> The women thronged to look, but never a one
> Showed sorrow in her eyes of steely blue.
> And little lads, lynchers that were to be,
> Danced round the dreadful thing in fiendish glee.(37)

The triteness of some of the diction in these lines does not destroy the point that custom and transference of frustrated emotional needs have produced monsters in American society.

In "To the White Fiends," McKay attempts to work with the ideas found in "The White House": hate is to be avoided, even when it is justified by dehumanizing conditions. By not hating oppressors, one can demonstrate his superior moral worth and shed some small degree of light "before the world is swallowed up in night" (38). "To the White Fiends" is not a successful poem, because the language in its advocacy of Christ-like forgiveness is trite and thus unconvincing. Still, McKay does achieve some interesting results with reverse connotation:

Think you I am not fiend and savage too?
Think you I could not arm me with a gun
And shoot down ten of you for every one
Of my black brothers murdered, burnt by you?
Be not deceived, for every deed you do
I could match — out-match: am I not Afric's son,
Black of that black land where black deeds are done? (38)

The intellectual and spiritual hypocrisy of a brutal racist society that judges individuals to be "savages" simply because they are black is the central issue of these lines. Here one also finds an attack upon that American egotism which allows the country to accept as reality its own propaganda and then to transmit its version of "truth" throughout the world. Americans, particularly when McKay wrote this poem, unquestioningly accepted the view that Africa was, always had been, and always would be a backward and a barbaric place; their books and films told them that the "natives" of "the dark continent" were murderous subhuman creatures.

McKay's own high regard for his poem "Harlem Shadows" was obvious as early as 1922 when he made it the title poem of the most important collection of his verse published in his lifetime. Although other critics have valued this poem equally, McKay's tendency to lapse into triteness and sentimentality that always threatens his poetry is especially noticeable in "Harlem Shadows." While the concept behind the poem is challenging, the poet's diction does not always meet the challenge. The device of elevating black prostitutes to the level of symbols of "my fallen race" is an example of McKay's daring and of his fondness for defying the Renaissance idea of "uplift." The success of "Harlem Shadows" resides in the poet's compassion and sympathy for the "little dark girls," and his movement into a symbolic statement about economic oppression within the American power structure. The most interesting thing about this poem is that it focuses almost exclusively upon the victims of racial discrimination rather than upon their oppressors. Although the concept of "The White House" lies behind "Harlem Shadows," McKay interprets that concept as an understood one. But the source of McKay's final failure in "Harlem Shadows" paradoxically lies in that same compassion and sympathy which gives the poem its main interest. In contrast to his vivid and controlled description in "The Harlem Dancer," the account of the suffering of the black prostitutes in "Harlem Shadows" degenerates into astonishing triteness:

> Ah, stern harsh world, that in the wretched way
> Of poverty, dishonor and disgrace
> Has pushed the timid little feet of clay
> The sacred brown feet of my fallen race! (60)

McKay was most likely to fall into such triteness when his emotions of anger and bitterness were not present to balance his unquestionably sincere sympathy. In "Outcast," which deals with the white rape of Africa and with its effect upon the historically displaced black man, McKay uses really effective language. The speaker proclaims that, if he were not held captive by the West, he "would go back to darkness and to peace" (41). The word, "darkness," when used to describe Africa, has the same ironic overtones which are present in "To the White Fiends"; and, by linking "darkness" with "peace," the poet emphasizes his irony. "Outcast" also confronts a problem intensely felt by several Harlem Renaissance figures and by a number of later Afro-American writers; as much as the speaker in "Outcast" would like to respond to some purely African culture, he is unable to do so:

> Something in me is lost, forever lost,
> Some vital thing has gone out of my heart,
> And I must walk the wall of life a ghost
> Among the sons of man, a thing apart. (41)

As mentioned earlier, McKay made a real attempt in his writing and in his personal life to return to Africa, only to discover that, however attractive and evocative, it was a foreign place to him. The black man in the West is truly an Ishmael. He worships "alien gods," but his soul longs to sing "forgotten jungle songs."

"Tiger" specifically attacks American imperialism, but McKay does not focus solely on Africa because Europe and Asia are regarded as being just as vulnerable to the power and ambition of the United States. This view of America as the originator and controller of an international social system based upon white supremacy and capitalism appears often in McKay, but in "Tiger" he also lashes the hypocrisy which masks American imperialism — all is done in the name of freedom and all "portends the Light of Day" (47). The controlling metaphor of the poem contains its own irony; when the white imperialist is compared to a tiger attacking an innocent black man, McKay's implication is that there are moral jungles more deadly than that physical one in Africa.

In a number of other poems in the "Baptism" and "Americana" sections, racial protest is not so overt, but blackness is still a major concern. For instance, the first twelve lines of "In Bondage" apparently reflect only a nostalgic longing for the simplicity of life in Jamaica, but the concluding couplet abruptly introduces the theme of racial discrimination: "But I am bound with you in your mean graves,/ O black men, simple slaves of ruthless slaves" (39). McKay's Victorianism is evident in the concept of universal human slavery, for he joins any number of nineteenth-century English and American poets in asserting that no man is finally free from pain, suffering, and death. However, he goes his own *black* way when he protests against the Negro's social and economic servitude; and this poem becomes a curious mixture of Jamaican nostalgia, stoicism, and black rage.

"On the Road" is a statement of McKay's sense of urban misery that is supported by a specifically black anger. The scene, a crowded railroad dining car, conveys a strong sense of discomfort and incivility. One feels the crowding, the rudeness, the lack of manners inherent in the setting. McKay's focus is, however, on those most affected by these conditions — the black waiters and porters. They are rushed and berated more than others; and, unlike the white passengers, they have no comfortable sanctuary to which they can flee when the ride is over. Inevitably, brutal dehumanization of the black is the result.

There is still one kind of McKay black poem that has not been discussed; "Africa," "The Wise Men of the East," "The Negro's Friend," and "The Negro's Tragedy" are all intensely philosophical, if not didactic, discussions of the inferior position of the black man throughout the world. In "Africa" and in "The Wise Men of the East," the concern is with the once powerful position of Africa in world affairs and its current status as a white-ravaged continent. In contrast to the writing of most advocates of black pride, McKay emphasizes the exploited present. Moreover, the tone of both poems is so peculiarly stern and chastizing that one almost feels that McKay is taking the position of an Old Testament prophet and is proclaiming that Africa's twentieth-century suffering is due to its past sins.

A much different criticism of McKay's race, or at least some of its most prominent spokesmen, is found in "The Negro's Friend" in which McKay directly engages the black intelligentsia who, he felt, are willing to sacrifice every meaningful advance of their people in the name of an unobtainable integration. The only real flaw of "The

Negro's Friend" is its overt didacticism. After a passionate and satisfying assertion that the only true road for the Negro to follow is the "classic" one of "fighting to the end," the poem argues that token integration is irrelevant to "fifteen million blacks" and that "the Negroes need Salvation from within" (51). "Salvation," however, should not be taken in a specifically Christian sense; rather, McKay means approximately what Malcolm X later was to advocate — the black community should organize itself economically and politically and not depend upon help from the surrounding white society. In essence, this poem is a plea for black pride and black power and an example of McKay's faith in black community solidarity.

In a different way, "The Negro's Tragedy" rests upon an assumption of black separatism and integrity. Until the sonnet's concluding couplet, the subject seems limited to black art. The thesis is simply that, since a Negro's suffering can only be understood by himself, no white man can hope to draw an aesthetically valid picture of the black soul: "So what I write is urged out of my blood./There is no white man who could write my book" (50). But the last two lines extend the poem's meaning "Our statesmen roam the world to set things right./The Negro laughs and prays to God for Light!" (50). Exactly whom the poet has in mind when he refers to "our statesmen" is a crucial question, but the context of the rest of the sonnet leads one to believe that McKay has the white representatives of America's political power in mind. It is true that McKay consistently attacked, in both poetry and fiction, the cynicism of an America which tried to export "democratic" principles to the rest of the world while maintaining racism at home. He saw both world wars as examples of this kind of hypocrisy. Of course, "our statesmen" could refer to those Negro leaders who, the Jamaican believed, had missed the real point of racial progress. Perhaps McKay is expressing his concern that the black intelligentsia will sacrifice black identity for purely materialistic gains.

Finally, the sonnet "Look Within" makes an interesting footnote to this discussion of McKay's specifically black verse. First published in *Catholic Worker* in February, 1945, the poem's tone and imagery, even though modified by McKay's conversion to Catholicism, are reminiscent of the 1920s black protest sonnets. World War II, like World War I, brought McKay's ideas about the essential hypocrisy behind United States foreign policy into sharp focus. In this poem and in the Eastman letters, the poet argues that the morality of an

American holy war against fascism abroad was compromised by its
racism at home. A pattern seems to emerge both in McKay's poetry
and in his letters to Eastman: because the war allowed him to reconcile many of his ambiguous feelings about the racial question, he
again directed his primary criticism at "the white house," rather
than at Negro intellectuals and political leaders. In "Look Within,"
the image of a corrupt and doomed white America is central;
however, in contrast to such sonnets as "The White House" and
"The White City," the vision of doom is specifically Christian. The
passion and the anger are that of the young Claude McKay, and only
the overtly Christian expression of his emotions reveal "Look
Within" to be a late poem.

Despite the frequent attempts of men like Max Eastman to view
McKay as primarily a lyric singer, his poetic reputation has always
rested primarily upon this body of unmistakably black verse; and it
will continue to do so. Uneven, often trite in form and diction and
overly didactic, these poems still express the rage of a proud and
eloquent black man; and in doing so they represented a necessary
and new direction for Afro-American poetry. The dialect verse of
Paul Dunbar was irrelevant to the turmoil of post-World-War-I
Negro life; Langston Hughes and Jean Toomer, who also represented major shifts in the emphasis of black poetry, were concerned
with their own aesthetic visions and modes of protest and did not
often utilize McKay's overt anger; but each created in his own way a
black art as meaningful and lasting as McKay's. Indeed, one could
argue that Hughes' poetry is a truer expression of Negro identity.

Still, the long-range importance of such poems as "If We Must
Die," "The White House," and "To the White Fiends" can be
quickly seen in any study of contemporary Afro-American poetry
and fiction.

Unquestionably, the main artistic failing of this verse is its frequent triteness of form and language — an understandable failing
because McKay was attempting something new and because he had
to establish new precepts and discard British tradition. Moreover, his
British education, the limitations of his imagination, and perhaps,
those of his taste caused him to imitate sometimes the worst of the
British poetic tradition. At its best, McKay's black poetry needs no
apologies; its passion and its vision give it an artistic conviction that
will last. Although one cannot help wishing that McKay had
attempted some of the innovations in black form and language that
dominate Hughes' poetry and McKay's own fiction, one would make

a serious mistake to minimize what he did accomplish. Even in the creation of this most important part of his total poetic output, he was not a great poet but was often an excellent one; and the role he played in the development of black American verse was invaluable.

In the remainder of the "Baptism" and "Americana" sections of *Selected Poems*, one finds expressions of the spiritual state of the speaker, proletarian protest, the misery of urban life, and longing for Jamaica. The poem, "Baptism," is the most famous, and the best, statement of McKay's conception of the test which brings maturity. The common practice seems to be to interpret it as a statement of the possibility of growth through specifically racial suffering, and such an interpretation is certainly acceptable. (Eugenia W. Collier believes that a *specific* racial snub — the treatment McKay received when he went to review a production of *He Who Gets Slapped* — inspired the poem.) However, as in the case of "If We Must Die," the sonnet's language makes other readings possible; and, since "Baptism" is hardly a call for immediate retaliation, it does not force the reader to look for any identifiable historic inspiration. The possibility that McKay did write it in reaction to racial injustice is strong, but it still can be regarded as relevant to any kind of real suffering.

The tone of "Baptism" is certainly in keeping with Victorian stoicism, and its imagery is essentially that of the Old Testament. The opening lines, "Into the furnace let me go alone; / Stay you without in terror of the heat, . . ." (35), grow out of the concept of the courageous individualist seen often in Victorian writing. Henley certainly could identify with such an individualistic theme; indeed, overtones of his "Invictus" are especially strong in the poem's middle lines:

> I will not quiver in the frailest bone,
> You will not note a flicker of defeat;
> My heart shall tremble not its fate to meet,
> My mouth give utterance to any moan. (35)

The last four lines, containing overtones of the Phoenix myth, are interestingly ambiguous:

> Desire destroys, consumes my mortal fears,
> Transforming me into a shape of flame.
> I will come out, back to your world of tears,
> A stronger soul within a finer frame. (35)

One can easily relate the conception of emerging from a test a better, stronger individual to the Phoenix myth as a supporting metaphor for the stoicism that dominates the rest of the poem; however, the reference to the consuming and transforming power of "desire" may lead elsewhere. One also wonders about the identity of the "you" who has stayed without and who exists in some vale of sadness to which the speaker must return. The concluding comment about "desire" reinforces the possibility, which exists throughout, of a sexual interpretation. In such a reading, "you" becomes a person who does not risk a total sexual commitment to another. In reference to the Henley-Kipling tradition, however, McKay could simply be distinguishing between those individuals who, like the speaker, "desire" to grow by confronting impossible problems, and those who avoid such challenge.

These concluding lines also work in a specifically black reading of "Baptism." Other McKay poems proclaim his "desire" never to shrink from the repression and injustice which he faces, and one of his key themes is that pride and identity are maintained only by such a direct response to white brutality. Members of oppressed minorities often find crutches to enable them to withstand the pain of their existence. Richard Wright makes this point in *Native Son* with his portrayals of Bigger's mother and her religion, his sister and her dream of respectability, and Bessie with her alcohol. Only Bigger, with his still emerging pride and individuality, has nothing to shield him from reality; and only Bigger attains stature at the novel's end. When read in a specifically racial context, "Baptism" can be seen as a forerunner of Bigger's story. The poem's narrator, like Wright's hero, "desires" to face the total meaning of his life and to grow from the encounter; but "you," like the people around Bigger Thomas, wants to be protected from the harshness of existence. The ambiguity of these concluding lines gives "Baptism" a multiplicity of possible meaning and makes it a most interesting poem. However one approaches the sonnet, it is vital to an understanding of McKay. There is no better statement of the most important aspects of his stoicism, and it may also be relevant to his attitude about confronting racial injustice — or it conceivably has overtones of a sexual philosophy. What is definite is that Claude McKay never held back from any "test."

McKay's involvement with proletarian thought lies behind two interesting sonnets, "The Castaways" and "The Tired Worker." "The Castaways," which was included in *Spring in New Hampshire,* opens with a tribute to the beauty of an urban park and shifts abruptly and effectively to a naturalistic description of some of capitalism's discards. "The Tired Worker," from *Harlem Shadows*, protests the tedium and misery of menial labor. The graphic picture of the castaways ("some withered women desolate and mean") that follows the traditional, almost trite, praise of butterflies, dandelions, and thrushes makes the sonnet's point quite effectively. In this context, "mean" is a particularly strong word; for any reader of George Orwell knows that poverty and neglect often produce mean-spirited people. McKay's point is that the decencies of civilization are luxuries that only the safe can afford; and this reality, more than the soiled clothing and the discolored faces, is what the speaker in the poem lacks the "strength . . . to see" in the closing couplet.

Sleep is "the tired worker's" only escape from a "wretched day" devoted to poorly rewarded, exhausting labor. Although the laborer possesses a "rebel heart," his daylight hours are "theirs" (79). The "they" refers to society's controllers who have devised a system which attacks the working man's mind by blocking any possible outlet for creativity or individuality; even the coming of night is an illusory escape, since the "dreaded dawn" reappears with shocking suddenness. At no point does the poem specify that the worker is black, and one senses that McKay's concern is for all laboring people. The concept of the spiritually killing quality of manual labor as it is known to be in a technological, assembly-line civilization could hardly be more contemporary.

Indeed, the sonnet shifts into a related theme in its last lines — the dehumanizing nature of urban life. Dawn means that once again the speaker will be forced to confront "the harsh, the ugly city" (79). McKay agrees with the nineteenth- and twentieth-century writers who have warned of the brutalizing effects of work which has no connection with nature (including human nature) and the soil. He expresses in other places a yearning to exist in harmony with a predominantly agrarian environment; however, he could never act upon that feeling. Such an existence had been possible in Jamaica, he believed; but the prospect of returning to that island outside the mainstream of literary and social innovation was distasteful to him. Still, the longing for an agrarian retreat is expressed in his work in attacks upon the harsh and brutal city and in affectionate reminiscences of his West Indian childhood.

In several of the remaining poems in "Americana," two sides of McKay's thwarted agrarianism coexist: a negative view of urban in-

dustrial life is balanced by a romanticized description of Jamaica.
For example, in "When Dawn Comes to the City," introductory
lines detail the ugliness of New York; the remainder of the poem
lyricizes the West Indies. Interestingly, McKay succeeds artistically
only in his initial negativism, for the lines recalling Jamaica are flat
and forced:

> And the tethered cow is lowing, lowing, lowing,
> And dear old Ned is braying, braying, braying,
> And the shaggy Nannie goat is calling, calling, calling. (63)

One feels that McKay, in this as well as in others of the *Selected
Poems*, is writing about Jamaica in the way he thinks a Romantic
poet should; but he does not always fail in this manner; in poems like
"Flame-Heart" and in *Banana Bottom*, the West Indies come alive.
In "When Dawn Comes to the City," the language in the opening
description of New York creates an immediate sensation of dullness
and lifelessness — the tenements are "cold as stone," the street cars
moan and grumble, and "dark figures" sadly stumble toward work
(63).

The theme of urban malaise is also found in McKay's poems
without any contrasting image of Jamaica. "Dawn in New York"
makes the same symbolic use of the approaching "new day" as "The
Tired Worker"; but "Dawn in New York" primarily creates a picture
of the essentially grotesque reality of the city instead of focusing
upon proletarian protest. The last line does introduce the theme of
the exploited worker, but otherwise McKay's concern is with the grotesque. The three lines satirizing white party-goers who are recover-
ing from their night in Harlem comprise the poem's best moment.

The short poem, "Rest in Peace," treats the city as a force destructive of all humanity, but especially of the black man. Proletarian
protest is also implied by an allusion to some "menial task." In its
treatment of black protest, urban brutality, and debasement of the
worker, the poem unites three of the four major themes of "Baptism" and "Americana." The body of the poem and the connotations
of the title imply that only death offers an escape from the types of
oppression with which McKay was concerned. In "Rest in Peace,"
"the city's hate, the city's prejudice" (77) turn life into a bitterly un-
rewarding existence. Again, McKay is giving "city" a broad applica-
tion, for this word refers to the totality of the white capitalistic structure. That structure, he feels with despair, inevitably dominates all
aspects of modern life.

II "Songs for Jamaica"

Nostalgia for the West Indies, which is used as a contrast in several of the "Americana" poems, is the major ingredient in the first section of *Selected Poems*. "Songs for Jamaica" romantically describes life in McKay's exotic, agrarian homeland. Interestingly, the dialect which characterizes the apprentice work in *Songs of Jamaica* and in *Constab Ballads* is dropped. Since the songs in this section of collected poems were aimed at an audience much different from the one addressed by the "Jamaican Bobby Burns," any language which McKay thought might seem difficult, or unsophisticated, was a liability. One common theme that emerges from this first section is a glorification of childhood innocence. McKay's vision of childhood as a time of purity unspoiled by passion and adult needs recalls the Romantic tradition of Wordsworth, Shelley, and Poe. A curious form of puritanism which is not uncommon in McKay's poetry but which is always artificial commonly appears in this initial section of *Selected Poems*. Female sexuality is often seen here as an almost supernatural danger to be avoided by the male at all costs.

Two poems, "Flame-Heart" and "The Plateau," largely transcend crippling puritanism and triteness and merit detailed discussion. "Flame-Heart," which is one of McKay's most evocative tributes to Jamaica, has a tone that is idyllic. The speaker's memories of nature and of joyous play have the kind of simplicity for which the Romantics often strive but rarely achieve. Perhaps more than any other of McKay's poems, "Flame-Heart" makes one understand why McKay often remembered Jamaica as an agrarian paradise. But the last stanza introduces the theme of a destructive sexual awakening that seriously disrupts the poem's harmony:

> I have embalmed the days,
> Even the sacred moments when we played,
> All innocent of passion, uncorrupt,
> At noon and evening in the flame-heart's shade. (13)

These lines seem especially out of place because the poem's refrain — "I have forgotten much, but still remember/ The poinsettia's red, blood-red, in warm December" (13) — implies a positive kind of passion. The poinsettia serves as a symbol of the island's natural beauty and warmth, but the emphasis placed upon "blood-red" seems to imply more.

"The Plateau" is an unjustly neglected poem. In it, civilized life is pictured as being destructive of man's healthy needs and desires; and any unnaturally inhibiting concept of "sin" or of sexuality is rejected. Passion is also given a positive emphasis in "The Plateau," for the lines not only depict a childhood scene which carries overtones of sexual maturation but contain also no complaint about the destruction of purity. In fact, the speaker's initial feeling of sexual awareness is remembered as a glorious experience. McKay analyzes the significance of a secluded place by the ocean for two Jamaican children and then for the narrator. For the first child, it simply meant natural beauty; for the second, it was a place to hide and watch "the happy lovers of the valley pass" (25). But one night on "the plateau," the speaker saw a moon, which awoke his latent passion and gave a purple beauty to flowers and the earth. The concept of an initial moment of sexual comprehension is loaded with much potential sentimentality. There are few things more difficult to write seriously about; but, through controlled imagery and form, McKay's technique succeeds. The traditional association of female sexuality with the moon establishes a universal imagery, and his vision of the earth's turning purple with passion is nicely understated.

Too often in "Songs for Jamaica" McKay does not exercise sufficient restraint. Puritanism and self-pity are the major excesses in this section of *Selected Poems*. "Flame-Heart," an otherwise sensitively written nature poem, is handicapped by an inexplicable turn to puritanism in the last stanza, where passion and sexuality are seen as inherently corrupt and destructive.

III   *"Amoroso"*

McKay's curious aversion to the sensual is even found occasionally in the love poems of Part IV, "Amoroso"; but, when this crippling puritanism is absent, McKay is a very good love poet. Although such poems as "A Red Flower," "Flower of Love," "A Memory of June," and "Flirtation" are based upon a quite positive attitude toward sexuality, "A Red Flower" and "Flower of Love" especially merit detailed discussion. McKay devotes the middle part of "A Red Flower" to a description of a woman's soul, but the first and last stanzas are variations of an extremely sensual image. This opening and conclusion are, in fact, highly reminiscent of the sensual love poetry of John Donne, Andrew Marvell, and other Metaphysical poets:

> Your lips are like a southern lily red,
>   Wet with soft rain-kisses of the night,

> In which the brown bee buries deep its head,
> When still the dawn's a silver sea of light.
> . . . .
> O were I hovering a bee, to probe
> Deep down within your scented heart, fair flower,
> Enfolded by your soft vermilion robe,
> Amorous of sweets, for but one perfect hour! (94)

Obviously, McKay understood the erotic effects achieved by suggesting sexual intercourse; and the elaborate central metaphor is worthy of Donne. As a result, the passion in this poem is not rejected — as in others — but is made even stronger by both control and originality. In "Flower of Love," the speaker recounts the beauties of each part of a woman's body and refers to her as the personification of his "loved South." After the introductory catalogue, the poem's eroticism is intensified:

> The portals of your sanctuary unseen
> Receive my offering, yielding unto me.
> Oh, with our love the night is warm and deep!
> The air is sweet, my flower, and sweet the flute
> Whose music lulls our burning brain to sleep,
> While we lie loving, passionate and mute. (97)

Discussing the woman's sex in religious terms again reminds one of Donne, and McKay's straightforward celebration of intercourse in these lines contrasts favorably with a poem like McKay's "Tormented." With no qualifications, "passionate" is an adjective of pleasure and beauty in "Flower of Love." Even the time immediately following the act itself is spoken of with tenderness — the speaker feels no need to plunge into a "silver stream" of purification.

Occasionally, McKay's love poetry illustrates an interesting combination of eroticism and the type of idealization common to Romantic verse. For instance, snow flakes linked together and falling gently to the earth arouse the speaker's sense of the idyllic in the first stanza of "The Snow Fairy." But, when his thoughts turn in the second stanza to a woman who, "with joy and passion all aflame," had spent the night in his bed, those entwined snowflakes acquire a new and decidedly sensual symbolic value (98). An opposite placement of effects is achieved in "Commemoration," the first part of which recounts the sensuality of a past love affair: "I never again shall feel your warm heart flushed,/ Panting with passion, naked unto mine"

(103). Suddenly, however, the woman is "transfigured" and
becomes "a miracle of godlike grace" (103). On this idealized note,
the poem ends.

The idyllic and the erotic are mingled in "Memorial," in which
the speaker remembers how the intensity of his desire virtually
robbed his beloved of her identity:

> You yielded to my touch with gentle grace,
> And though my passion was a mighty wave
> That buried you beneath its strong embrace,
> You were yet happy in the moment's grace. (104)

A thrill still comes when he visualizes her "clean brown body,
beautiful and young" (104); but, he responds equally with these impressions to her purity that raised her above "coarser forms of love."
Even in moments of unrestrained passion, he "touched [her] flesh
with reverential hands" and saw her as a precious jewel that required
careful handling (104). Despite some triteness in the opening stanza,
McKay's treatment of this duality is successful. An obvious implication is that the moments of supreme sexual enjoyment enhanced his
appreciation of the woman's near divinity.

It would be surprising and disappointing if McKay did not deal
with interracial love in "Amoroso." The treatment of that theme in
"One Year After" is especially intriguing; in its first stanza, the inevitability of failure for a black-white sexual relationship is attributed not to society's pressures but to the speaker's own black
pride and integrity. McKay's thesis that a black man betrays his race
— and himself — when he turns to a white woman for sexual fulfillment is as contemporary as Eldridge Cleaver, Imamu Amiri Baraka,
or Don L. Lee. The obvious implication that individual and racial
loyalties cannot really be separated reflects Claude McKay at his
angriest. Even before the speaker faced the treachery inherent in his
devotion to an oppressor, he refrained from any total commitment:

> Not once in all our days of poignant love,
> Did I a single instant give to thee
> My undivided being wholly free. (105)

Since he was always torn between an instinctive blackness and a
powerful attraction to this woman, the initial stanza has a strong un-
dertone of anger — bitterness toward the temptress, and an even
more intense disgust with self. Yet, when the speaker announces in

the second stanza the probability of more such liaisons, there is no apology.

There is confusion inherent in any attempt to put together the two parts of "One Year After"; but, when the speaker describes his inability to resist additional entrapments, he explains his self-contempt in the first half of the poem. Now, since he is consciously aware of the racial treachery involved, he must feel special shame at the prospect of future weakness. The fact that his shame is hidden in the closing lines is simply added evidence of a lack of control. Moreover, inevitability is always a convenient, if not a convincing, excuse. When read in this way, "One Year After" is an impressive accomplishment; and, since McKay lets the speaker judge and condemn himself, no authorial comment is required. The psychological suffering of a weak black man who nevertheless has a sense of racial loyalty is subtly and indirectly portrayed.

Although the best of McKay's love poetry is impressive, he especially proves himself to be a master of erotic metaphysical imagery. This controlled eroticism is, in itself, strong protection against the excessive sentimentality that occasionally plagues his work. One must be especially impressed by his ability to incorporate the sensual into verse that is otherwise highly idealized. Finally, "One Year After" also establishes him as both a prophetic voice in the development of black consciousness and as a master of the artistic investigation of complex psychology. After "Baptism" and "Americana," "Amoroso" is easily the most impressive part of *Selected Poems*. In fact, strictly in terms of aesthetic achievement, its best work is equal to that in the two middle sections, "Baptism" and "Americana." The metaphysical imagery in "A Red Flower" and "Flower of Love" may not be inherently black, but it is masterfully handled; and the part of McKay the poet that desired to be "universal" must have been pleased with it.

IV   *"Different Places"*

Part IV, "Different Places," consists of poetic tributes to Russian civilization, the city of Barcelona, and North Africa. The poems reflect the influence in the 1920s and early 1930s of three radically different civilizations upon McKay. The Jamaican's early commitment to Marxism, his response to the exotic and the classical, and his desire to find in North Africa a black sanctuary are major themes in this verse. The two Russian poems especially demonstrate a universal response, for Lenin's appeal is no greater than Russia's unique mixture of Eastern and Western cultures. In fact, nearly all the complex feelings which the Soviet Union aroused in its black visitor are suggested in "Moscow." The opening line implies sympathy for those people whose world ended with their revolution. McKay was disturbed in 1922 and 1923 by the oppression experienced by the Czar's loyalists, but he later described such oppression as a major factor in his disillusionment with Marxism. His universal humanitarianism would never permit him to accept discrimination against anyone; and the term, "enemy of the state," was repugnant to all that he believed. Oriental exoticism becomes the next emphasis in the poem: Moscow is a "bright Byzantine fair" which fills the air with "amorous sounding tones like passionate lyres" (83). Then, a subtle transition leads to praise of Lenin and his government; McKay talks of the luxuriant colors of Moscow; and he then says: "And reigning over all the color red"(83). The last stanza is orthodox Marxist verse.

Discrimination against Russia's one-time aristocracy caused him concern in 1922 - 1923, but not enough to destroy his sense of the enormous promise and potential of the young Soviet Union. His autobiography reveals that McKay was then personally impressed by Lenin, as well as by Trotsky, and that he thought it yet possible for Russia's new order to produce a workers' paradise. "Moscow" is evidence that one cannot accept the Jamaican's assertions to Eastman in the late 1930s and the 1940s that he had never believed in the Marxist cause. In fact, he had placed a great deal of hope in the revolution; and, as a result, his disillusionment was all the more bitter because this optimism had existed. Still, the opening stress in the poem on the suffering of the Czarists foreshadowed McKay's inevitable failure as a good Marxist. It is also interesting, and perhaps significant, that the artistic level of the first half of "Moscow," especially those lines stressing Eastern exoticism, surpasses that of the last half. The superiority of his description of the purely picturesque tends to support McKay's contention that he was a poet before he was a political being.

In "St. Isaac's Church, Petrograd," the poet explains how the awesome structure of the church gave him a new sense of the power of Christ. An important distinction needs to be made: McKay expresses no loyalty to Christianity as an institution. In fact, the poem implies a separation of Christ and the church hierarchy. McKay's symbolic point is that Christ personifies "man's Divinity" which makes possible a creation as impressive as St. Isaac's Church. Man's creative energy is god, and a cathedral is really the human celebration of its own divinity. Christ becomes, therefore, a representative of all poets, architects, and other artists. Overtones of Dostoevsky appear in the rest of McKay's theory, for he implies that a relationship exists between mankind's suffering and its power to produce lasting beauty. Christ on the cross is "the marble Man of Woe," (84) and His church developed from the suffering of the Russian masses. It seems strange that McKay never pursued this concept of art derived from suffering in connection with black art, but the emphasis in his black poetry on anger and hate may explain his apparent oversight — or he might have thought rage to be more stimulating than passive suffering. At any rate, one wonders if St. Isaac's Church caused McKay to express his ideas about the artistic riches inspired by Czarist oppression openly to his revolutionary hosts; if so, their reactions must have been memorable. The poem is an impressive accomplishment, for it explores in very few lines the interrelationship of suffering and human divinity which makes possible all great art; and a subtle imagery, instead of overt didacticism, is the basis of this exploration.

"Barcelona" sings the praises of virtually every aspect of that city. Its people are "primitive" in the sense McKay admired — their lives are lived in harmony with the rhythms of nature. The corruptions of Western civilization do not seem to have touched this natural order and beauty. Their unrestrained celebrations best illustrate the integrity of their lives. Two other characteristics of Barcelona are of equal importance — the physical nature which surrounds the city, and its dens of "vice." The stanza concerning nature is traditional and somewhat derivative, but the tribute to Barcelona's red-light district is original and personal. Vice, as celebrated in Barcelona, is "eccentric," "savage," "abysmal," and irresistible. In the city's "bottoms sinister and strange," one sees scenes from Goya and also practically every conceivable rejection of respectability (85). Barcelona brings together people from all over the world; and, since it allows them to discard all inhibitions, its environment is a triumph of things sensual. None of this harms the primitive purity of the Spanish peasants; but it could not, to McKay, since Western capitalism and industrialism were all they had to fear. The poem's final stanza summarizes the unique sensuousness and capacity for life of the "queen of Europe's cities."

In "Tetuan," Spain's exotic beauty is attributed to its mingling of Western and African traditions. On the continent,

> Africa's fingers tipped with miracles,
> And quivering with Arabian designs,
> Traced words and figures like exotic flowers. (87)

McKay's concept of the European peasant's primitive joy is also described in "Barcelona" and his response to Spain does seem to have been deeper than his feelings toward any European country for the reasons discussed in "Tetuan." Its rural inhabitants were isolated from, and thus uncontaminated by, white Western civilization; and the North African influence was strong. In this poem, McKay is most concerned with North Africa's "gift" of a sense of the exotic and mysterious to Spain.

"A Farewell to Morocco" is the poet's tribute to the continent he was about to leave in order to return to America; but, after studying the letters which the Jamaican wrote to Eastman between 1930 and 1934, it is impossible to read this poem without an almost painful sense of irony. McKay revealed to his old benefactor that he felt lonely (almost insanely lonely) and separated from the intellectual currents of his time during the Moroccan years. After the apparent failure of *Banana Bottom,* the need and the desire to reestablish himself as a writer *in America* became more intense. Ironically, McKay's negative emotions find no expression in "A Farewell to Morocco"; and, as in "Tetuan," North Africa is praised for its mystery, its power of enchantment, and its erotic appeal. Why the speaker must depart this "wistful and heartrending earth," is left unexplained: he merely vows never to forget it. One does not question the sincerity of this poem. North Africa undoubtedly would give anyone with McKay's kind of black consciousness a strong emotional identification. Still, his identification with Africa was almost certainly not as strong as he would have wanted. For whatever insight it might provide, McKay's language in "A Farewell to Morocco" is trite and forced; and the poem is not a good one.

The five poems in "Different Places" illustrate the diversity of setting and cultural influence to which Claude McKay could, and did, respond. He was a complex man who was always driven by equally intense intellect and emotion. Because Marxism became the most bitterly disappointing of all the false ideals to which McKay devoted parts of his life, and because his lasting greatness lies in his artistic expression of black pride, the greatest irony in "Different Places" is that the two Russian poems constitute the aesthetically strongest part of this section of *Selected Poems* and that "A Farewell to Morocco" is the weakest.

V *Conclusion*

For a final evaluation of Claude McKay the poet, it is useful to turn to Melvin B. Tolson's review of *Selected Poems*. To Tolson, the "logic of facts" separated McKay and other Harlem Renaissance poets from "the New Poetry and Criticism" of the 1920s.[12] The work of Jean Toomer seems to bring this generalization into question; and, to the degree that "the New Poetry and Criticism" simply implied innovation and rejection of restrictive and traditional poetic form and language, so would that of Langston Hughes. But Tolson is correct about Claude McKay, for his poetry does seem to have come from a different world than the work of Pound, Cummings, and Stevens — and, in fact, it did. By the "logic of facts," one assumes that Tolson is referring to McKay's special burdens of protest against white oppression, to the virtual absence of Afro-American poetic tradition, and to McKay's lifelong allegiance to British literary traditions of the nineteenth century. McKay had to be concerned with expressing a black anger against injustice and with creating something to replace the dialect verse of Paul Dunbar. Radical innovation in form was not, then, one of McKay's concerns; in fact, he was suspicious of it. As mentioned, one often wishes that it had been different and that McKay could have seen a correlation between technical innovation in poetry and blackness. But the facts are, as Tolson says, that ". . . McKay's radicalism was in content — not in form."[13] Still, the "content" of McKay's specifically black poetry was instrumental in shattering "the mold of the Dialect School and the Booker T. Washington compromise."[14]

Though Tolson never directly says so, one assumes Tolson is implying that McKay's kind of "radicalism" made it easier for the later Afro-American poets who were concerned with the "New Poetry"— and because Tolson himself is a prime example of the post-Renaissance innovators, his review of *Selected Poems* is a significant tribute to the writer of "If We Must Die." The McKay heritage to black poetry is then doubly meaningful: his rebellion against the plantation school resulted in a liberation whose dimensions he did not foresee. In the 1940s, Tolson's artistic world was not so alien from that of Pound and Cummings; and Ishmael Reed completes, of course, the movement into experimentation. What McKay undoubtedly did hope for, if not foresee, was the angry black poetry of Baraka and Lee; and his contribution to that school is clear.

Apart from McKay's overtly black poetic contribution, there is more: some interesting proletarian verse, expressions of spiritual anguish, and some fine metaphysical love poetry, for example. The best of the poems in "Amoroso" have never been sufficiently appreciated. Finally, in "St. Isaac's Church, Petrograd," McKay developed an intriguing concept of the relationship between art, religion, and human suffering; and the several dimensions of his personality and interests had positive aesthetic results.

In his novels, he was able to be revolutionary in both form and content. When he wrote *Banana Bottom*, he reached the peak of his literary promise. For that reason, the three novels are ultimately more rewarding than the poetry. Nonetheless, *Selected Poems* is both a landmark of Afro-American writing and evidence of an ability to handle with success diverse themes and subject matter. *Harlem Shadows* was the book which firmly established McKay as a Harlem Renaissance figure. Unlike *Home to Harlem*, it pleased virtually everyone in the Renaissance establishment. Obviously, for several key people, an unrealistically limited perception of Claude McKay resulted from it. Partly because of that misconception, the book gave its author a position of influence in the Negro literary movement of the 1920s which he might well not otherwise have held.

CHAPTER 3

The Novels: Instinct versus Intellect

I The Critical Reception of McKay's Novels

IN a 1928 review in *The Crisis*, W. E. B. DuBois dismissed *Home to Harlem*: "For the most part [*Home to Harlem*] nauseates me, and after the dirtier parts of its filth I feel distinctly like taking a bath."[1] McKay's novels have always generated controversy and misunderstanding, and one easily understands why the "old guard" Negro leaders were antagonistic to McKay's first novel. *Home to Harlem* was not representative of what they had wanted the Harlem Renaissance to be; it seemed the opposite of their spiritual uplift program because of its lovingly detailed concentration on black "low life" and because it idealized the black masses instead of the "Talented Tenth." To many, the book seemed an example of Van Vechtenism (DuBois had disliked *Nigger Heaven* too),[2] but a more contemptible one since it had been written by a black writer. Undoubtedly, the novel's popularity disturbed people like DuBois; they must have felt that the white reading public was responding to McKay because he seemed to be verifying all of their stereotypes.[3] In fact, in an excellent recent study, *Harlem Renaissance*, Nathan Irvin Huggins restates much the same argument: ". . . the novel became a best seller precisely because it pandered to commercial tastes by conforming to the sensationalism demanded by the white vogue in black primitivism."[4]

The initial controversy and misunderstanding surrounding *Home to Harlem* — as well as his other two novels, *Banjo* and *Banana Bottom* — has continued in McKay criticism. For instance, David Littlejohn in *Black on White* (1966) fully accepts DuBois's evaluation of *Home to Harlem* as degrading sensationalism;[5] and he dismisses McKay, the novelist, as a "small-souled declamatory propagandist."[6] Obviously the belief persists that McKay, in an

69

attempt to capitalize upon the *Nigger Heaven* vogue of the black man as an exotic primitive, libelled his race as untalented denizens of a world of vice and promiscuity. In addition, McKay's fiction has frequently been dismissed as technically artless; as Stephen Bronz asserts "[the novels and stories] . . . are choppily written melanges of sketch, remembrance, and polemic, showing little sign of critical editing. Still, if the novels and stories are weak as literature, they are not devoid of sociological interest."[7] Bronz's evaluation is surprising because he is extremely sensitive in many ways to McKay's art.

However, the criticism of McKay increasingly reflects an awareness that the three novels deal with much more than sensationalism, that they are not racially degrading, but that they illustrate McKay's continuing effort to express a theory of "cultural dualism" in an aesthetically valid manner. Moreover, some critics have indicated that the last novel, *Banana Bottom*, represents considerable artistic progress in this effort. Three critics, in particular, have described the unifying thread in McKay's novels as the theme of "cultural dualism" and argued convincingly for the artistic growth exemplified in *Banana Bottom*. Robert A. Bone, in *The Negro Novel in America* (1958), develops these two ideas in a convincing, but abbreviated manner. Two recent McKay critics, Kenneth Ramchand in *The West Indian Novel and its Background* (1970) and George E. Kent in his article, "The Soulful Way of Claude McKay," (1970) have enlarged upon this central theme in the three novels and upon McKay's artistic development.

The assertion that "cultural dualism" is McKay's continuing theme simply means that black pride was the motivating ideal behind all three novels and that he was developing a thesis of positive black and of negative white values. What blinded such a man as DuBois to what McKay was doing was McKay's rejection of the entire notion of black uplift, for all three novels propose that the black masses possess the inherent strengths requisite for spiritual progress. One does not have to disparage DuBois too strongly for this error; there are elements in McKay's elaboration of his thesis that are essentially romantic, and DuBois' intellect and unceasing political involvement in the advancement of his race could certainly have made him impatient of this kind of romanticism. Ironically, the young McKay viewed DuBois with considerable admiration: "[*The Souls of Black Folk*] shook me like an earthquake. Dr. DuBois stands on a pedestal illuminated in my mind. And the light that shines there comes from my first reading of *The Souls of Black Folk* and also from the *Crisis* editorial, "Returning Soldiers," which he published when he returned from Europe in the spring of 1919."[8] On a young man afire with the passion of black pride, the eloquent *Souls of Black Folk* could have had no other effect.

As discussed in Chapter 1, the principles and factors underlying McKay's association of positive values with blackness and of negative qualities with whiteness are hinted at in two articles written at widely separated points in his career: "A Negro to his Critics" (1932) and "Boyhood in Jamaica" (1953). Again, the novelist's association with black working-class life in America had given him an impression that the Negro masses possessed a unique spontaneity and ability to enjoy "physical and sensuous delights" without restraint or guilt; and McKay's contempt for white materialism grew throughout his stay in America. On the most basic level, the conflict in the three novels centers around black characters who are attempting to retain their ability to respond instinctively to such "natural" pleasures as sex, comradeship, and music and dance in the face of a pervasive materialism that threatens all such "simple" delights. In *Home to Harlem*, this conflict is limited to America; but, in the last two novels, it is given worldwide applicability.

While one can read McKay's novels as three versions of the same story of black "innocents" at war with all aspects of white civilization, they are not that simple. As shown in Chapter 1, McKay's attitude toward white civilization was never one of total rejection and hatred, for something in him responded favorably to "the steel-framed poetry of American cities" and to America's "mighty throbbing force, its grand energy and power and bigness. . . ."[9] Moreover, McKay was never such a romantic that he believed that a complete "innocent" could survive in this century. What finally emerges from the novels is a sense of the awesomeness of Western culture and of the corruption at its heart. Whites in America and Europe have sold their souls to materialism; and, through their imperialism, they threaten to engulf the nonwhite world in their soulless sterility.

Related to the shallowness of white materialism is the viciousness of white racism. More directly and more defiantly than any other voice of the Harlem Renaissance, McKay attacked white racism. Still, as the endings of *Banjo* and *Banana Bottom* make clear, there are things to be gained from white civilization. The writers that Ray of *Home to Harlem* and *Banjo* admires are white writers, as are, for that matter, most of the literary figures to whom McKay pays tribute in *A Long Way From Home*. McKay's final message, as personified

in Bita of *Banana Bottom,* is that the black man of the world must
strive to utilize whatever is valid in white civilization without being
corrupted by its materialism. As George E. Kent succinctly remarks,
"Absorbing what was inescapable in Western culture and what must
be mastered in order to live in the 'modern' world, he [McKay]
attempted to develop from within. That is, he wished to draw into
himself strands of Western culture that agreed with his own
rhythms, but not to be shook by its devitalizing vibrations — its
tendency to be the blow-fly, corrupting impulses derived from
healthy and close association of man with his fellows and with the
deepest rhythms of land, water, and sky."[10]

McKay's belief that Western culture was corrupted by
materialism and racism did not imply that its universal,
humanitarian voices had to be rejected by nonwhites. The legacy of
the great British and Russian poets and novelists, as well as that of
the best contemporary American white writers, need not be dismissed as foreign by the black man. In *Banana Bottom,* Bita Plant
renounces the life planned for her by white missionaries in order to
marry a Jamaican peasant and live with him in her native village.
She does not, however, stop reading William Blake and Pascal. The
novel's final image of Bita comfortably at home with her peasant
husband and reading Pascal's *Penseés* is McKay's most successful
aesthetic depiction of an ideal black community solidarity combined
with appreciation of white Western thought. Bita does not separate
herself from her native village, and she would not dream of "uplifting" intellectually her husband Jubban.

McKay did not quickly and easily arrive at this final position. It is
relevant to point out that only one year separated *Home to Harlem*
(1928) and *Banjo* (1929) and that four more years elapsed before the
appearance of *Banana Bottom* (1933). In the first two novels, McKay
struggles philosophically and artistically; and the best evidence of
the struggle is in the characterization of Ray (McKay's obvious
spokesman). Much, if not most, of the artistic difficulty in *Home to
Harlem* is related to McKay's use of Ray to voice his own still
somewhat uncertain ideas about blackness and whiteness. In *Banjo,*
Ray is much more certain about his philosophy of cultural dualism,
but his repeated lectures on the subject make one doubt that McKay
was completely comfortable with the thesis. Between *Banjo* and
Banana Bottom, McKay obviously arrived at a racial position with
which he was at ease; and this newly found ideological maturity
enabled him to write a novel aesthetically much superior to the first

two. Most importantly, he dropped the device of having a character verbalize his ideas: Bita Plant in *Banana Bottom* does not say what she is; she enacts her ideas of herself. She *is* what Ray has been talking about throughout the first two novels.

It has been charged that McKay's final concept of black identity is ultimately white-defined.[11] Some critics have said that he attributed certain characteristics to whites — materialism, sexual inhibition, greed — and then claimed their opposites — affinity with nature, sexual naturalness, and generosity — as aspects of the black soul. His concept of black soul grows out of a negative definition of whiteness and is, thus, ironically white-controlled. While there is undeniably some truth in this argument, it is not an entirely fair criticism. The charge must be answered, however, in individual discussions of the three novels; but this problem is one that virtually every Afro-American writer who has attempted to define a black consciousness has faced.

II   Home to Harlem

"Oh, to be in Harlem again after two years away. The deep-dyed color, the thickness, the closeness of it. The noises of Harlem. The sugared laughter. The honey-talk on its streets. And all night long, ragtime and 'blues' playing somewhere, . . . singing somewhere, dancing somewhere! Oh, the contagious fever of Harlem. Burning everywhere in dark-eyed Harlem. . . . Burning now in Jake's sweet blood. . . ."[12] This expresses Jake's feelings upon his return to Harlem from World War I. Almost immediately he encounters a bewitching prostitute, sleeps with her, and discovers the next morning that she has returned his money. At this point, Harlem is an oasis of pleasure and sensuousness for Jake; it is the one place in the world in which he can be free and comfortable. Europe was war and racism; white America is cold materialism, oppression of the black man, and a kind of spiritual sterility. But on Jake's return, and for most of the novel, Harlem is a haven that is almost "pure" because it is comparatively uncontaminated by guilt, lust for power, or by materialism. Harlem is the "womens," "chocolate, chestnut, coffee, ebony, cream, yellow" (32); and each color has its own distinctive promise of erotic pleasure.

On one level, McKay's vision of Harlem is a decidedly adolescent male fantasy. The female characters in *Home to Harlem* (and *Banjo* for that matter) are depicted largely as objects of gratification for the central male characters. Even Ray, who in *Home to Harlem* is virtually rendered impotent by his intellectual confusions, is not totally untouched by the pervading sensuality of Harlem. In *Banjo*, he recounts an experience in Paris; he had been modeling nude when his mind had wandered, and he "was lost away back in Harlem, right there at the Sheba Palace, in a sea of forms of such warmth and color that never was seen in any Paris studio." Ray became sexually aroused and was forced to flee from the podium.[13]

Even after Jake is separated from the generous prostitute without having learned her name or address, he is not overly disturbed. He spends the rest of the book searching for her in a leisurely fashion and finds much diversion from other "womens." However, this sensuality presents its own problems and complications. In *A Long Way From Home*, McKay comments that certain critics felt he was "imitating" Hemingway in *Home to Harlem*.[14] McKay expresses his admiration for Hemingway: the author of *The Sun Also Rises* "shot a fist in the face of the false romantic-realists,"[15] and he expressed for the first time in American literature "the hard-boiled contempt for and disgust with sissyness expressed among all classes of Americans."[16] But McKay also denies any direct influence by Hemingway on his work; he asserts that "any critic who considers it important enough to take the trouble can trace in my stuff a clearly consistent emotional-realist thread, from the time I published my book of dialect verse *(Songs of Jamaica)* in 1912, through the period of my verse and prose in *The Liberator*, until the publication of *Home to Harlem*."[17]

Obviously, McKay felt that the term "emotional-realist" applied both to Hemingway's work and to his own; and he also believed it to be a healthy reaction against the "false romantic-realists." Although one finds a confusing terminology in these statements, the essential point that McKay is making is clear — both he and Hemingway dealt with "low life," the socially unacceptable, in what they considered a "realistic" manner. But whether he intends to admit it or not, McKay is admitting that his presentation of the "underworld" is not objective — he is an "emotional realist." McKay's presentation is the key to DuBois' objection to *Home to Harlem*; for McKay, like Hemingway, romanticizes his social outcasts. Also much like the Hemingway of *The Sun Also Rises*, he especially idealizes the male characters and depicts a masculine world in which women exist both as objects of sexual gratification and as obstacles to true male comradeship. The concept of female depravity is most explicitly stated in the following passage: "From experience in seaport towns in

America, in France, in England, he had concluded that a woman could always go farther than a man in coarseness, depravity, and sheer cupidity. Men were ugly and brutal. But beside women they were merely vicious children. Ignorant about the aim and meaning and fulfillment of life; uncertain and indeterminate; weak. Rude children who loved excelling in spectacular acts to win the applause of women" (69).

This attitude is more than a little similar to that of the world of *The Sun Also Rises* in which Jake and Bill can be content for a while on an all-male fishing expedition; Brett always beckons them back with disastrous consequences; but they nevertheless answer her call. In Hemingway, and in McKay, the male characters' disgust with the females is always a temporary thing; for perverse as women may be at times, Brett Ashley and "the sweet browns" of Harlem are too alluring to be denied for very long.

Despite the complications, Jake's goal is to enjoy the sensuality of Harlem (without the "womens," "there ain't no life anywhere"), while keeping the turmoil produced by female "depravity" to a minimum. Ultimately, he decides that the best way to accomplish this objective is to find one good, loyal woman and to settle down permanently with her. For this reason, he attempts to find the "tantalizing brown" he had met on his arrival home; but, as mentioned, Jake is constantly distracted from this search by the sensuality that pervades the very air of Harlem. His concept of the "depravity" of women is no protection from this distraction.

Harlem is no Eden. Men make fools of themselves, and they even kill each other there in senseless fights, as well as in downtown New York or in Europe. Violence, petty jealousies, and enmities exist in Harlem as they do universally. But, until the end of the novel, it is still the place where Jake feels most free and most alive. As illustrated by the prostitute's returning his money, it is possible in Harlem to experience sexual pleasure that is not based exclusively on materialism. Moreover, in frequent passages that must have made DuBois cringe, Jake and his friends assert the black woman's superiority in matters of sex. One can, of course, argue that McKay was catering to Van Vechtenism and to white stereotypes of black sexual prowess. In fact, it is difficult to refute totally such a criticism.

Yet, there seems to be more involved. To McKay, sex is not only an essential need; it is one of the most intense of pleasures. McKay relates Negroes' capacity for sexual enjoyment (even the most cursory reading of his work will show that this generalization is not

limited to black women) to the relative black freedom from con-
tamination by corrupt white values. Since the white world makes
everything else dependent on materialism and the lust for power, the
whites treat sex in the same fashion and, thus, pervert it. To the
degree that black characters are unspoiled by these perverse white
values, they can respond more spontaneously and naturally to sexual
pleasure. Thus, Harlem is an oasis of sexuality, where one can hope
to escape the white world's perversion of this necessary pleasure.
The "depravity" of "the womens" does occasionally result in com-
plication, but certainly not often enough to cause a mentally and
physically healthy black man like Jake to refrain from the pleasures
they can provide.

Yet it must be pointed out that Harlem is a community surrounded by white society; moreover, white invasions of the black
cabarets occur regularly in the novel. Thus, the black integrity of
Harlem is constantly in danger of being compromised by perversion
from white values. The characters in *Home to Harlem* are aware of
this threat; in fact, Jake comments to himself early in the novel:
" 'Same old New York. But the ofay faces are different from those
ovah across the pond. Sure they is. Stiffer. Tighter. Yes, they is
that' " (25). Ray declares later that ". . . even New York, passing its
strange thousands through its great metropolitan mill, cannot rob
Negroes of their native color and laughter" (191). As positive as
Ray's statement is, it nevertheless demonstrates an awareness that
the larger white society of New York is always potentially at war with
black values. As will be shown, that white threat finally destroys
Harlem's "sweetness" for Jake. Both Jake and Ray are aware of the
white threat; and the central section of the novel (Book II) in which
Jake goes to work as a railroad porter and is forced to leave Harlem,
and even New York, is important primarily as a means of introducing
Ray into the novel and of illustrating exactly what McKay is attacking — the cold exploitative nature of white commercialism and
its effects upon the black man.

The climax of Book II's dramatization of white oppression comes
when Jake and Ray and the other black rail employees are forced to
spend the night during a Pittsburgh stopover in quarters provided
for them by the railroad company. The cots, which the white-owned
company deems adequate for the men, are infested with bugs. To escape the misery of "the Pennsy bug house," Jake and Ray go with a
friend to a "little open-all-night place"; there they are offered
opium; and Jake immediately accepts: " 'I ain't got the habit, boh,
but I'll try anything once again' " (149). Ray declines, and he and

Jake eventually return to the railroad sleeping quarters, but not before Jake acquires a few more packets of opium. Jake goes to sleep immediately; but Ray, tortured by the bugs, cannot. Lying miserably awake, he curses himself for leaving his home in Haiti, curses his race for being exploited, and curses the white race for exploiting it. Ray's bitterness demonstrates McKay's awareness of the self-hatred which a minority group member can so easily develop in a racist, oppressive society. Certainly, then, the "antagonist" is identified in *Home to Harlem*.

The conclusion of the "Pennsy bug house" incident intensifies the theme of self-hatred. Finally giving up on any other means of going to sleep, and dwelling on ". . . the filthy fact of the quarters that the richest railroad in the world had provided for its black servitors" (156), Ray takes all the opium in Jake's coat; he experiences a series of erotic hallucinations during the night; but the next morning he has to be rushed to the hospital. At work on the railroad the next day, Jake thinks of Ray's experience and declares: " 'We may all be niggers aw'right, but we ain't nonetall all the same' " (159). The feeling of being "nonetall" almost killed Ray; and McKay's point is unmistakable: if the brutality of a white-imposed environment could do this to Ray with his intellectualism (and with his peculiar form of puritanism that will be discussed later), a similar self-destruction might easily befall any ordinary black man.

Generally, but much more subtly than in this Pittsburgh section, McKay makes his point about white oppression throughout Book II. The detailed descriptions of the menial, degrading labor of the railroad workers and of their resulting petty squabbles dominate the rest of the railroad episodes, and Ray's verbalizing of his constantly evolving philosophy of antiwhite materialism then carries the remainder of this middle section of the novel. The petty jealousies and bickering among the porters are underscored in the "war" between Jake's and Ray's crew and their despotic chef, who is characterized as a black man who is trying to be white.

The Pittsburgh sequence; the characterization of the chef; and, as will be discussed later, Ray's rejection of white materialism and his struggle to accept his blackness represent a negative white set of values with which Harlem's and Jake's blackness contrasts. The novel's structure is not so loose as has generally been suggested: Books I and III focus on Jake and are essentially concerned with the nature of blackness; Book II concentrates on Ray and subordinate characters in an attack on white, oppressive materialism.

The criticism of this novel has generally not done justice to the

characterizations of Jake and Ray; Jake in particular has been the
victim of oversimplification. The usual approach to Jake is to refer to
his instinctual simplicity and to let it go at that. For instance, Bone
asserts that Jake "represents pure instinct"[18] and "is the typical
McKay protagonist — the primitive Negro, untouched by the decay
of Occidental civilization."[19] Nathan Irvin Huggins believes that
"Jake is a child-man, having the simplicity and innocence of Mark
Twain's Nigger Jim, and the childlike openness and spontaneity of
E. E. Cummings' Jean Le Negre."[20] "Instinct," "innocence," and
"spontaneity" are certainly terms that can and should be applied to
Jake; he is, after all, the embodiment of that purity which the all-
powerful white world is attempting to destroy. There is ample
evidence in the novel that a spontaneous innocence is one of Jake's
most distinguishing characteristics. He makes love freely and rather
indiscriminately — and, as a result, he gets a venereal disease. Of
course, he reacts to the venereal disease in the way he reacts to most
things — he sees it as a minor inconvenience, not to be overly
worried about. In fact, when Ray scolds him for not having used a
contraceptive device, Jake refers to such protection as "kill-joy
things" (206). In the pursuit of pleasure, it is obvious that he wishes
to feel as free as possible.

In terms of Jake's day-to-day existence, he approaches most things
in the same way as sex — confidently and instinctively. Where
McKay describes Jake's life as "a free coarse thing," he is utilizing
the same device of reverse connotation that is so effective in much of
his poetry. "Coarse" is to be taken here as a positive adjective,
meaning essentially what the critics mean when they talk about
Jake's casual devotion to sex and related pleasures. Yet, those critics
who focus upon Jake's sense of moderation in spite of his love of
what American puritanism would label "vices" are also correct. His
experience with venereal disease is perhaps the one exception to
Jake's sense of proportion, of not going too far. As McKay states,
"Gambling did not have a strangle hold upon him any more than
dope or desire did. Jake took what he wanted of whatever he fancied
and . . . kept going" (269). Jake is willing to try opium or virtually
anything else "once again," but he knows when to stop; he is responsible to himself. The contrast between Jake's "instinctive" moderation and Ray's near death as a result of an overdose of opium is
strong.

Thus, "spontaneity," "instinct," and "naturalness" are undeniably major aspects of Jake's characterization and of the positive
concept of blackness which he personifies; but these characteristics

are not the only elements either of Jake's being or of McKay's vision of black pride. When Huggins remarks of Jake, "he just does not want to hurt anybody, that is his singular moral judgment,"[21] he is only partly correct. Although a sense of decency and humanitarianism is an integral part of Jake's personality, it is not his only morality. Most importantly, Jake acts on a set of values based strongly on black pride — in a quiet, but firm way, Jake is determined never to be "nonetall." He declared a "separate peace" from World War I when he recognized that blacks were not to be fighting men in the battle of "self-determination," but only manual laborers.

Pride in his own worth also explains Jake's attitude toward labor unions. At the beginning of the novel, he quits a job when he learns that he has been hired as a scab (". . . it ain't decent to scab . . .") (48). Nevertheless, he refuses to join any union because of the racism inherent in all labor organizations. These sentiments toward the war and white-dominated unions assuredly are not the views of a total "innocent" or "exotic primitive."

Another example of Jake's pride is his refusal to live as a "sweetman" in the presence of continual opportunity. Despite the fact that men who live off the earnings of a woman are considered by many as an "exotic aristocracy" in Harlem (82), Jake will have no part of such an arrangement. This insistence upon not being supported by any woman is the beginning of Jake's inevitable break with Congo Rose, the cabaret entertainer with whom he lives for a while. A second factor in the breakup between Jake and Rose is equally significant: despite Rose's predilection for sadomasochistic acts, Jake is determined not to participate in any of them with her. To Rose, love without such perversity is not love. Finally, when Rose is able to exasperate Jake sufficiently for him to slap her twice "full in her face," she believes that their relationship is now perfect; but Jake is so sickened that he leaves Rose permanently.

Here McKay touches on what becomes a major theme in *Banjo*. Since Jake to some degree personifies racial integrity, his abhorrence at the perversion of "natural, normal" sex must be seen as an aspect of McKay's concept of positive blackness. Rose, with her masochism, must be seen, then, as a perversion of black identity. In *Banjo*, McKay simplifies the issue by associating sexual perversions of all kinds (including sadomasochism) with a group of white intellectuals. The characterization of Rose, in part, illustrates one of McKay's main theses — the black community is constantly in danger of having its most basic virtues perverted by surrounding white values. One answer, then, seems obvious to the charge that McKay was personifying, in characters like Jake, a concept of positive blackness derived simply by inverting white values. If Jake were Nigger Jim, the charge would be irrefutable; but "spontaneity" and "instinct," while certainly a major part of his characterization, are not the whole of his character. In conscious decisions, he rejects the war, labor unions, and the parasitic life of a "sweetman" because they are incompatible with black pride. In a recent article, Richard K. Barksdale sees Jake as the one symbol of constant "order" in a world dominated by disorder and chaos.[22] Barksdale is correct, and that "order" originates in Jake's black pride and constant refusal to compromise his integrity.

Even to the degree that Jake's characterization is based upon a reversal of alleged white values, there seems, nevertheless, no necessity to lay the blame totally at the door of any desire of McKay's to capitalize upon Van Vechtenism. The black man in America, as well as the black writer, has rarely escaped some control by the predominant white society. Ralph Ellison has written a long novel in which the main black character simply assumes one identity given to him by the white society only to have to exchange it for another; at the end, after rejecting all these roles, Ellison's hero settles for invisibility. To ask the black artist to operate with a total independence from white influence is, then, to ask a great deal indeed, especially McKay, who was working virtually without any tradition of "independent" Afro-American literature. Most certainly, the fiction of Charles Chesnutt, Paul L. Dunbar, and the earlier black writers are so white-influenced that they could have been of virtually no help to McKay. McKay undoubtedly believed that he had seen in black life a healthy contrast to white corruption.

To the degree that McKay romantically exaggerates this contrast (as he did), he can also be viewed as having done essentially what any number of twentieth-century American writers have done. Moreover, Congo Rose, the cabaret girl in Home to Harlem, shows that the black consciousness has not emerged unscathed; and the ending of Home to Harlem, as well as all later McKay fiction, reinforces this fact. Still, one could charge that a formula which equates "instinct," "spontaneity," emotional and sexual "naturalness" with blackness, and which considers perverted materialism and intellectualism with whiteness condescends to the black mind. To some degree, it does; and the characterization of Ray demonstrates that McKay realized it. Of course, the same formula makes McKay vulnerable to the accusation of reverse racism. Littlejohn, for instance, calls McKay's fiction "incoherent black-racist propaganda."[23] McKay might well have answered Littlejohn by stating, honestly and correctly, that the necessity for establishing a literature of black pride was worth the risk of appearing to some a reactionary racist.

At any rate, Ray not only demonstrates McKay's concern about these problems but also foreshadows his solution to them. Ray enters *Home to Harlem* by giving Jake his first lesson in black history when he tells Jake of the pride that blacks should feel in Toussaint L'Ouverture, Abyssinia ("Abyssinia, oldest unconquered nation, ancient-strange as Egypt, persistent as Palestine, legendary as Greece, magical as Persia"), and Sheba ("And Sheba reminded them that she was black but beautiful. . .") (135 - 36). But, as the "Pennsy bug house" episode demonstrates, Ray does not have his black pride nearly so well established as his history lesson indicates. In the remainder of Book II, Ray begins to resolve his mental conflicts and uncertainties about his own blackness and his relationship to his race; and Jake's friendship is vital in this development.

Some information about Ray's background is relevant, for it strongly parallels McKay's. Ray was born in Haiti, an island, and first came to the United States when an adult. The son of a formerly prominent official in the government of his native Haiti, he had been enjoying a Howard University education until United States imperialism deprived him of it. As a result, Ray has ample reason to dislike American imperialism, and he is already struggling to accept his race and its heritage. But his intellectualism and suspicion of his own and others' desire for sensual pleasure make this acceptance difficult. Huggins correctly asserts that Ray ". . . has been made impotent by thought";[24] but this assertion needs explanation. Ray, from the beginning, understands power and all its ramifications; and he is personally and intellectually aware that his race does not have it. This sense of racial powerlessness translates into a personal inability to act, primarily because Ray initially despises the blacks for lacking power. At one point, he informs a co-worker on the train that " '. . . God is white and has no more time for niggers than you've got for the chef' " (176). Of course, then, he despises himself and puritanically restrains all impulses which he feels that his own race indulges in too freely. As a result, Jake's friendship provides a dual service for Ray — it enables him to get close to *one* representative of the black masses and to see his worth, and these experiences free Ray from his own imitation-white puritanism. A key incident in this learning process is a scene in a brothel to which Jake has taken Ray, and where he lectures the latter on the liberation inherent in sexual fulfillment.

Another element in Ray's uncertainty is simply an intellectual confusion which, in a significant long passage, McKay analyzes as a part of the *weltschmerz* (world-sickness) of the times. Wanting to be a writer, Ray realizes that, because of "the great mass carnage in Europe and the great mass revolution in Russia" (225 - 26), he is living at the end of an era. Moreover, "Ray was not prophetic-minded enough to define the total evil that the one had wrought [World War I] nor the ultimate splendor of the other [the Russian Revolution]" (226). Most significantly, he believes that the white writers whom his education had taught him to admire have become irrelevant because of the totality of world change. A few new voices promise fresh inspiration — James Joyce, D. H. Lawrence, Sherwood Anderson (227); but, of the old literary gods, "only the Russians of the late era seemed to stand up like giants in the new" (228). Without models and with the old masters displaced, Ray is uncertain that he can create art out of ". . . the utter blinding nakedness and violent coloring of life" (228). All he is certain of is that, if he can, it will be a bitterly realistic art.

Subsequently, Ray verbalizes the idea that his white-structured education is no longer relevant and has, in fact, unfitted him for the "new era." Seemingly, Ray has located the villain — white power in its guises of materialism, imperialism, and education. He is also starting to get to the necessary acceptance of his own people, but he never fully does in *Home to Harlem*. In *Home to Harlem*, one is left with a feeling of uncertainty and confusion concerning Ray because the ending of Book II is probably the biggest artistic flaw in the novel. McKay arbitrarily introduces the nice, educated black girl Agatha who wants to marry Ray; but Ray refuses because he sees marriage as a trap that would make him ". . . one of the contented hogs in the pigpen of Harlem, getting ready to litter little black piggies" (263). Obviously, some racial self-hatred is the cause of this attitude. When Ray leaves for Europe to escape Agatha, his departure occasions several expressions of conflicting emotions concerning Harlem and his race. In resorting to the device of having Ray leave for Europe and by attempting to tie all the loose ends of his characterization together in about six summary pages, McKay fails to end the confusion in this section of the novel. Since a critical commonplace is that Ray is McKay's alter-ego and since the idea needs little support, the confusions that plague Ray at the end of *Home to Harlem* were McKay's own; moreover, for this reason he is finally unable to resolve them satisfactorily. But Ray has grown in the course of the novel; and, in *Banjo*, the extent of his growth becomes evident.

Most certainly, Ray's growth would not have been possible without the association with Jake, as has been observed; but Ray also has had an effect upon Jake. For instance, the mere sight of Ray's Agatha revives in Jake a desire not only to find his lost prostitute but to marry her; this situation begins Book III. From the start, Harlem in Book III is not what it was in Book I; and the desperation about safety there makes even Jake uneasy. Billy Biasse, a friend of Jake, insists that it is now dangerous not to be armed in Harlem; and he describes a senseless interracial brawl that he saw occur for no reason. In explanation, Billy says," 'Wese too thick together in Harlem. Wese all just lumped together without a chanst to choose and so we natcherally hate one another' " (285). Jake feels the claustrophobic pressure and accepts the loan of a gun from Billy.

Harlem, then, is no longer the Eden it was in Book I; and this time the difficulty is not the "womens' " fault. One can guess whose fault McKay thinks it is—the white society that has packed blacks together in Harlem so thickly that they cannot breathe easily. One probably has here a miniature version of the larger one in *Banjo*, for a small black community is encircled and suffocated by the powerful white world. McKay, who never makes this point as clearly as he might have in *Home to Harlem*, probably did not do so for the same reason that he dealt inadequately with Ray at the end of Book II.

When Jake does find his "little brown" again, she is with his friend Zeddy. Jake, initially not realizing this fact, simply claims her. Later, Jake and Zeddy confront each other in a crowded cabaret; and Zeddy pulls his razor on Jake (ironically, earlier in the novel, Jake has prevented Zeddy from committing murder). When Jake faces Zeddy down with the revolver from Billy Biasse, Zeddy shouts that Jake was a cowardly deserter in the war and retreats. Jake now has his girl (symbolically named Felice); but he has new problems.

The threat of white authorities learning of Jake's desertion is not easily resolved, and Jake and Felice plan to leave for Chicago after one more night of "jazzing" at the Baltimore cabaret. Thus, Jake is driven out of Harlem finally by the threat of the white-power structure; and the tone of the last few pages of the novel reveals an increasingly intense bitterness about black-white relations. Earlier in the novel, the Baltimore has been closed by a police raid, but Felice, who tells Jake that it is now reopened, declares: " 'White folks can't padlock niggers outa joy forever . . .' " (336). Finally, McKay launches into an authorial aside during a description of the black dancing at the Baltimore:

Haunting rhythm, mingling of naive wistfulness and charming gayety, now sheering over into mad riotous joy, now, like a jungle mask, strange, unfamiliar, disturbing, now plunging headlong into the far dim depths of profundity and rising out as suddenly with a simple, childish grin and the white visitors laugh. They see the grin only. Here are none of the well-patterned, well-made emotions of the respectable world. A laugh might finish in a sob. A moan end in hilarity. That gorilla type wriggling there with his hands so strangely hugging his mate, may strangle her tonight. But he has no thought of that now. He loves the warm wriggle and is lost in it. Simple, raw emotions and real. They frighten and repel refined souls, because they are too intensely real, just as a simple savage stands dismayed before nice emotions that he instantly perceives are false (337 - 38).

This passage is a tribute to that "simplicity" and "naturalness" about which McKay critics write; moreover, it seems in its tone to be a rather desperate attempt by McKay to accept fully these qualities as inherently black. But, more importantly than any of this overt primitivism, it is a statement that the black psyche is more complex than superficial glimpses indicate and that the white world is determined not to go beyond superficial glimpses. Thus, interracial understanding seems impossible — a point which is one message toward which the novel has always been heading.

III Banjo

As in *Home to Harlem*, McKay opens *Banjo* by introducing a character whose main thematic function is to personify black values. Banjo (Lincoln Agrippa Daily, a native of the American South) is to the second novel what Jake was to the first. The standard critical assessment of Banjo that he represents "instinct," "spontaneity," and "sensuality" is, in large part, accurate. In fact, readers who might be bothered by implied condescension or reverse racism in McKay's formula of black-white values in *Home to Harlem* would probably be even more disturbed by *Banjo*. The sterility and the perversion of materialistic white culture, while a major theme in *Home to Harlem*, are not in the first novel repeatedly summarized, analyzed, and denounced; but they are in *Banjo*. Also, it is easier to overlook the distinctly conscious black pride and the shrewdness in the characterization of Banjo than in that of Jake. This potential oversimplification is a real danger in *Banjo* because McKay *tells* the reader constantly that Banjo is a man of "instinct" and "naturalness."

Black music, which figured strongly in the background of *Home to Harlem* as a symbol of black identity, is brought to the forefront in *Banjo* and is utilized as a major motif. Banjo's very name (or nickname) is meant to increase his symbolic value as the epitome of blackness. In fact, such symbolism is another example of McKay's love of utilizing the very stereotypes that outraged DuBois, Locke, and others of the Harlem Renaissance intellectuals: "The sharp, noisy notes of the banjo belong to the American Negro's loud music of life — an affirmation of his hardy existence in the midst of the biggest, the most tumultuous civilization of modern life" (49). Moreover, McKay, as if to challenge the "new Negro" exponents directly, creates the character Goosey, whose sole function is to expound the "uplift" philosophy.

McKay knew that his novel was weakly plotted (the subtitle is "a story without a plot"), but the fragmentary plot concerns Banjo's attempt to organize a black orchestra comprised of the beach boys of the Marseilles waterfront.

Even more than in the case of Jake's search for Felice, the "plot" gets sidetracked again and again because the beach boys themselves, not their potential as musicians, are what is really vital in the novel. The Marseilles setting and the gang of black vagabonds who lead a hand-to-mouth existence on the waterfront add a universal dimension to *Banjo* that *Home to Harlem* lacked. Malty, Ginger, Dengel, Bugsy, Taloufa, and Goosey represent all the key geographical areas inhabited by the black race (the West Indies, Africa, America), and the diversity of their personal experiences and ideas adds to McKay's goal of representing black universality. In the words of Jacqueline Kaye, *Banjo* ". . . seeks to arrive at the common black denominator, the essential Negroness, the equivalent of the Negritude to be generated by the poetry of Francophone blacks."[25]

Also typical of McKay's love of antagonizing the American black intellectual establishment is his selection of Marseilles as the meeting place for this fictional Pan-African conference, as well as his lingering affectionately over the details of its prostitution and general "vice." When Banjo meets up with the beach boys at the beginning of the novel, an episodic account of their largely "instinctive" and "natural" life is underway. Athough Banjo is seemingly a representative of total "instinct" and "spontaneity," he is not, but McKay makes it easy to misjudge him as such. For instance, in his introduction of Banjo, McKay calls him ". . . a great vagabond of lowly life" (11). Then the author gives his character speeches like the following: " 'The joy stuff a life ain't nevah finished for this heah strutter. When I turn mahself loose for a big wild joyful jazz a life, you can bet you' sweet life I ain't gwine nevah regretting it. Ise got moh joy stuff in mah whistle than you're [sic] got in you' whole meager-dawg body' " (24).

Banjo's "joystuff" is that same ability to appreciate life, and especially sex, that is possessed by Jake in *Home to Harlem*, and he is not just bragging. When Banjo arrives in Marseilles, "*instinctively* he drifted to the Ditch [locale of the city's "vice"], and as *naturally* he found a girl there" (13, italics mine). This particular girl, who is white, turns out to be no great bargain since she deserts Banjo as soon as he runs out of money. On the strength of his "joystuff," Banjo attempts to reclaim the white girl early in the novel and suffers a knife wound from her pimp for his effort. Walking through the streets nursing his wound, he is "rescued" by Latnah, a mysterious woman of mixed nonwhite blood; and he is taken home by her — to stay as long as he wants. Latnah has always refused to give herself sexually to any of the beach boys. That night, Banjo muses about his persistent, if unpredictable, luck with "the womens."

But, like Jake, Banjo possesses a conscious black pride and a shrewdness that enables him to survive in an overwhelmingly white world. Surprisingly, in fact, Banjo's antiwhite sentiments are expressed, at times, more vindictively than Jake's ever are. Banjo does not consistently maintain an antiwhite philosophy; but, when it does emerge, it is bitter. For instance, Banjo is even bitterer than Jake about the American Negro's treatment during World War I. At one point in the novel, the beach boys are given a free meal by a ship in port; Banjo refuses to partake when he overhears an officer of the ship refer to the blacks as " 'a damned lot a disgusting niggers' "; and he later upbraids his companions for accepting such condescending philanthropy. The bitterness behind such a speech is made extremely painful near the end of the novel when one learns that Banjo had seen his brother lynched in the South.

Moreover, Banjo is not consistently antiwhite. He gives five francs to a hungry white boy; and Bugsy, who is a consistent hater of all whites, tells Latnah that the incident is proof that Banjo loves white people more than he does his own race. Latnah happens to be susceptible to Bugsy's argument because, at this point, Banjo has deserted her to return again to the white girl, Chere Blanche, who left him at the opening of the novel. McKay makes it abundantly clear that Bugsy is wrong, for Banjo is simply instinctively generous and is "color-blind" in matters of human suffering and sex. Banjo, the McKay male ideal, indiscriminately enjoys "the womens" whenever he can and whoever they are; but the criticism of an adolescent male dream world is again applicable. Of course, Chere Blanche leaves Banjo again; and, when he sees Latnah afterward, he exclaims, " 'How could I evah love white moh'n colored? . . . White folks smell like laundry soap' " (255).

Thus, there are more complexities in the characterization of Banjo than may at first appear and more than most critics have recognized. He is assuredly the personification of black soul and black music, which means an emphasis upon "instinct" and "spontaneity." He consciously and bitterly resents white racists, believes that they constitute the majority of white people (" 'the wul' safe foh democracy is a wul' safe foh crackerism' "), and is ready to fight if and when they push him too far. But he will aid a white person, or anyone, in need. Banjo's attitude toward whites reflects, therefore, a curious combination of shrewd wariness, potential hatred, and humane impulse; and his attitude is probably not a great deal different from McKay's own.

With the characters of Banjo, Latnah, and the beach boys, McKay has potentially a good picaresque novel. He is as adept at utilizing the exotic background of Marseilles as he was of Harlem in *Home to Harlem*. But it is not long before Ray, who is more mature and angrier than in *Home to Harlem*, enters the novel and begins to harangue so interminably that his lectures overwhelm the setting and the other characters. Still wishing to become a writer, Ray has spent the time since his abrupt exit from Harlem traveling throughout Europe looking for material. This search is the attraction of a place like Marseilles — Ray still feels that, when he develops his art, it will realistically depict "lowlife." He has come to recognize more clearly than ever the evils of white materialism and imperialism. And when the novel opens, he is almost, but not quite, ready to accept proudly the black races of the world as they are. At the end of the novel, he has overcome this last remaining hesitation because of the inspiration he derives from Banjo and the beach boys. A more mature Ray with a wealth of new experiences since he left

Harlem has intriguing possibilities; but, with far too few exceptions,
McKay has Ray lecture the other characters (and the reader), instead
of placing him in dramatic situations and having his ideas emerge
through his actions.

Ray is even more obviously the spokesman for McKay in *Banjo*
than he was in *Home to Harlem*, and perhaps this fact explains the
author's inability to work him into the art of the novel. Ray's intellectual confusions about accepting his blackness hamper *Home to
Harlem*; and, ironically, when these uncertainties are virtually
resolved in *Banjo*, he spoils the narrative flow with his lectures. One
feels that, in the second novel, McKay finally attains his own intellectual vision and proclaims it to the world. The feeling persists
also that he is not yet totally comfortable with the vision precisely
because of his need to state it so frequently. Only when in *Banana
Bottom* he sensitively and subtly dramatizes his ideas about black-
white values does one feel that McKay is really philosophically comfortable. At any rate, Ray's theory of the corruption and perversion
of white capitalism and materialism is hard to miss in *Banjo*.

Another target of Ray's lectures is the American black intellectual
establishment. Goosey serves as an excellent foil for Ray, as well as
Banjo; but Banjo's verbal jabs at the theory of black progressivism
are basically instinctual, and Ray's are the result of a conscious
philosophy. Thus, Goosey (and by implication, the Harlem intellectual) receives negative criticism from both Banjo and Ray. One of
the most interesting exchanges between Ray and Goosey results
when the latter expresses horror at Ray's announcement that he intends to write about black life on the Marseilles waterfront: " 'But
the crackers will use what you write against the race!' " Ray replies
that, if they do, he cannot be bothered about it, for he must be concerned only with telling a good story. When Goosey then asks what
possible artistic beauty can be found in the dirt of the waterfront,
Ray replies: " 'Many fine things come out of dirt — steel and gold,
pearls and all the rare stones that your nice women must have to be
happy.' " This comment then leads to a discussion of the black press
and black society, and Ray attacks both: " 'I am fed up with class.
The white world is stinking rotten and going to hell on it.' " McKay,
this time, does allow Goosey to score a last point by denouncing the
"United Snakes": Ray immediately seizes the metaphor.

Until Goosey's moment of triumph, one cannot help feeling that
in this passage McKay is answering the attitude of the Renaissance
establishment. What is especially interesting in the exchange is Ray's

declaration of his greater commitment to artistic integrity than to racial advancement, for McKay made a similar choice of art over proletarian propaganda. McKay's rejection of the role of proletarian writer and this speech by Ray are indicative of a sense of self and of an individualism that always were integral parts of McKay's philosophical makeup. As will be discussed later, this individualism bothers such a critic as George E. Kent who would prefer McKay to have been a uniformly militant spokesman on black issues. Yet, despite Ray's statement of the necessity that art totally eclipse racial consciousness and despite McKay's individualistic nature, McKay definitely does not submerge his racial consciousness in his novels, in his nonfiction, or in most of his poetry. Perhaps to express that personal independence, McKay gives Ray some speeches that do not harmonize perfectly with his own racial consciousness; but, Ray's (and McKay's) final conceptions of art are rooted in the values of the black masses. One could debate about whether or not a black writer ever can or should totally subordinate color consciousness to artistic purpose — or if there really is any inherent conflict between the two. Whatever the answer one gives to such questions, it is highly ironic that it is in *Banjo*, by far the most consciously propagandistic of McKay's novels, that he has Ray state such an opinion.

The question of Ray's relationship to the proletariat reappears in the novel with results that must have greatly shocked Max Eastman and McKay's old *Liberator* colleagues. Ray asserts that, in politics, he is indeed committed to the proletariat; but he still insists that he despises "the proletarian spawn of civilization." He flippantly asserts that politics has nothing to do with "faith" or reason (106). Since Ray is McKay's "mouthpiece," it should have been abundantly clear that the writer was never going to make a good Marxist. Moreover, the Ray of *Banjo* is determined to have no illusions about any white people. For instance, when a French student attempts to get him to agree that blacks are generally well treated in France, Ray replies that, to the degree the statement is true, it is only because France does not have a real Negro population. He then points out that the French record of racial tolerance in Africa is nothing to brag about — a passage that anticipates James Baldwin's ideas about Europe and race in *Notes of a Native Son*.

Three main principles distinguish Ray's "lectures" in *Banjo*: his individuality or sense of self; his view of the universality of white prejudice and corruption; and his constantly evolving sense of black identity. As mentioned, the first and third of these beliefs do potentially conflict; and George E. Kent criticizes McKay most severely as a black spokesman on this precise point: "This romantic stance of the individual nourishing himself on the poetry of existence intrudes upon McKay's very serious moments and attenuates their quality. It seems to make for a kind of romantic egoism that produces solitariness where kinship with larger issues and people is required, and a startling myopia. The result is divisive tensions; rhythms of a natural Black style, romantic rebellion, bohemian aestheticism, egoism, and a sharp realistic social vision, uneasily commingling."[26] Obviously, if one wants McKay to be a 1920s Imamu Amiri Baraka, this attack is fully justified. Indeed, McKay's own life is proof that he did have trouble reconciling his sense of self-worth with his membership in any group. Yet, one must stress again that McKay's fiction, with its underlying concept of a uniquely black art, clearly anticipates the emergence of such a writer as Baraka.

In *Banjo*, however, Ray and McKay have no trouble being consistent about the perversion of Western materialistic culture: "Business! Prejudice and business. In Europe, Asia, Australia, Africa, America, those were the two united terrors confronting the colored man. He was the butt of the white man's indecent public prejudices. Prejudices insensate and petty, bloody, vicious, vile, brutal, raffine, hypocritical, Christian. Prejudices. Prejudices like the stock market — curtailed, diminishing, increasing, changing chameleon-like, according to time and place, like the color of the white man's soul, controlled by the exigencies of the white man's business" (193). One could quote similar passages almost indefinitely.

Despite Ray's having made an intellectual acceptance of his race, he still has some difficulty in emotionally relating to his blackness. Part of the problem is what Kent calls the "romantic stance of the individual," but it is primarily Ray's uncertainty about whether his white-oriented education and intellectuality will allow him to participate fully in black life. What ultimately happens, however, is that the example of Banjo and the beach boys enables Ray to overcome this uncertainty. Here again, McKay has the potential for a quite interesting novel — if he would show this process, if he would dramatize it — and for developing an aesthetically satisfying work of fiction. Curiously, however, even though Ray repeatedly engages in picaresque adventures with the beach boys, the effect on him would not be evident if he did not relate it to the reader — which, of course, he does. Life with Banjo and the gang on the Marseilles waterfront even allows Ray to come to a final thesis about the future of black art. Another example of the real frustration in dealing with *Banjo* is that Ray's final visions of universal black brotherhood and of a new black art are so contemporary that the book can never be dismissed as unimportant; but, because McKay fails to dramatize adequately Ray's attainment of these principles, one finds it impossible to feel comfortable with the novel as a novel.

Still, one comprehends certain aspects about black art and black brotherhood because of Ray's (or McKay's) speeches about them as they develop almost simultaneously (ultimately the new art is dependent upon the sense of brotherhood); and the catalysts for both theories are Banjo and the beach boys. Ray's progression toward his final beliefs concerning the black masses and the new black art is clearly outlined. One clue to his philosophical direction comes when, in a storytelling session with some of the beach boys, he recounts an African folktale, followed by a speech praising African sculpture. Then, about two-thirds of the way through the novel, Ray declares to a mulatto student that any black cultural renaissance must be founded upon the black masses and that white education can only be a handicap in arriving at this new folk art. Ray then advises that, as models, the student look not only at Irish and Russian literature because of their incorporation of the wisdom of the peasants, but also at African dialects and " '. . . be humble before their simple beauty instead of despising them' " (208 - 09). Here is the essence of the "new art" theory — it must have its roots in the masses and be as independent as possible of the imperialistic white culture.

Then, in a long meditative passage near the end of the novel, Ray puts everything together. He first reaches an epiphany about the effect upon him of association with Banjo and the beach boys: "He had associated too closely with the beach boys not to realize that their loose, instinctive way of living was more deeply related to his own self-preservation than all the principles, or social-morality lessons with which he had been inculcated by the wiseacres of the civilized machine." Moreover, he realizes that he enjoys the company of Africans because they ". . . gave him a positive feeling of wholesome contact with racial roots" and that he gets the same "positive feeling" through association with the beach boys. Specifically, he is aware that, from the beach boys, he hears a purity of black speech and absorbs a "natural gusto for living," neither of which can ever be felt through association with the "Negro *literati*." Rather abruptly, Ray then reaches the conclusion that is critical not only to *Banjo* but also to *Banana Bottom* — he can merge instinct and intellect. Ray is finally at peace with himself, and the reader is relieved that the lectures and philosophical speculations have ended.

One must in fairness to McKay point out that he does attempt at times to present dramatically and symbolically this theme of "cultural dualism," and Bone's analysis of such attempts is excellent. He points out that an American steamship company frequently mentioned in the novel is called "the Dollar Line," he emphasizes that the "brutality of the French police toward the beach boys" increases in the last third of the novel, and he calls attention to the "Blue Cinema" and to the French chauffeur episodes.[27]

The "Blue Cinema" chapter is especially worth discussion. As mentioned, a group of European and American followers of an internationally famous Satanist arrives in Marseilles and immediately becomes involved with Ray and the beach boys; this involvement comes about because a female disciple of the Satanist remembers Ray from a period during which he did nude modeling in Paris. The leader of the cult is known for his sadomasochistic sexual rites and is looking for some unique form of perversion on the Marseilles waterfront. The woman remarks shortly after her reunion with Ray that he " '. . . has posed in the nude for my friends and he was a perfectly-behaved *sauvage*' " (213). Of course, McKay himself often uses words like "savage" with positive connotations; but the woman is simply being condescending and is, of course, mentally reflecting upon all the myths of black sexuality.

All that her group can think about doing in Marseilles is to go to "the Blue Cinema," a pornographic film. One of the white younger members of the group, an American, refuses to go if both the woman and Ray are present (a nicely ironic comment upon white schizophrenia about race and sex). Without the young American, Ray and the Satanists proceed to the film; Ray is immediately repulsed, but the woman watches with fascination until a curtain is suddenly drawn back revealing a group of Chinese waiting to give a live performance with some of the local prostitutes; then the woman screams. McKay is getting all the mileage he can out of the central irony of the episode; and the final turn comes when the young American who refused to join the party disappears and is later found ". . . on a lonely quay behind Joliette, stripped of everything and wearing a dirty rag of a loin-cloth for his only clothing. The sudden and forced reversal to a savage state had shocked him temporarily daft" (218). When the Satanists meet Banjo, they are instantly intrigued and beg him to join them on their excursion. When Ray fervently begs Banjo not to go, he does; but he shortly returns and is exceedingly reluctant to discuss his experiences with the Satanists. The most satisfying prose in *Banjo* occurs in impressionistic passages. For instance, McKay sets up an analogy of racial conflict to a bullfight and compares "the composite voice of the Negro — speech, song, and laughter" to the red cape that baffles and maddens the bull, or the white man (314). In describing the beauty of a sexual experience between Ray and Latnah, McKay writes: "Peace and forgetfulness in the bosom of a brown woman. Warm brown body and restless dark body like a black root growing down in the soft brown earth. Deep dark passion of bodies close to the earth understanding each other. Dark brown bodies of the earth, earthy. Dark . . . brown . . . rich colors of the nourishing earth. The pinks bring trouble and tumult and riot into dark lives" (283 - 84). Finally, however, passages like these and episodes like "the Blue Cinema" are not enough to save *Banjo* artistically: they only make one aware of the novel one *might* be reading.

Increasing the sense of aesthetic failure is the novel's ending; and, for varying reasons, virtually every McKay critic finds it defective. After McKay reaches the conclusion that Ray can now merge intellect and black instinct, Ray decides to "go vagabonding" with Banjo. Their plans are uncertain except that they intend to travel extensively; live a hobo life; and, except as temporary objects of pleasure, exclude women from their future. This decision is comparable to having a Hemingway have Jake and Bill decide to make a permanent thing out of their fishing expedition. In some ways, such a decision would be a nice idea, except that the entire focus of both *Banjo* and *The Sun Also Rises* has shown that such escape is impossible. Also, the ending is, of course, another example of McKay's adolescent male fantasy world.

But there are other, more important, problems with the ending. The reader is not prepared to accept Ray's assumption of the vagabond life because he has not been shown how Ray can utilize his intellectual powers in such an existence. Finally, *Banjo* has demonstrated so strongly and so repeatedly the universal, inescapable nature of white oppression and imperialism that one wonders just how the two characters hope to escape by hoboing around the world. Ray has said so often that the corrupt white man has his hands on every square inch of the globe that one believes him; therefore, one is unable to accept the ending as being a valid answer to any of the issues the novel has raised.

The ending of *Banana Bottom* is somewhat similar; but, in the later novel, it is logically and aesthetically acceptable because the rest of the narrative anticipates Bita Plant's "retreat" as an inevitable act. This ending in *Banjo* confirms what has been said before: McKay could never utilize the character of Ray with any aesthetic success. Ray's harangues throughout *Banjo* and his retreat at the end leave the reader with the uneasy feeling that McKay had so recently worked out his cultural dualism theory that, forcibly presented as it is in *Banjo*, he was still somewhat insecure about it.

IV   Banana Bottom

It is at least interesting that McKay turned to his native Jamaica for the setting of his best novel. *Banana Bottom*, in fact, is the pinnacle of McKay's literary career; on the surface, a quiet, almost pastoral, work, this novel makes all the points about black pride and white corruption that dominate his other prose, as well as his protest poems. It avoids both the temptation of overt lecture that plagues *Banjo* and the patronizingly "stoical" approach to Jamaican peasant life that is so annoying in many of the *Songs of Jamaica*. McKay had artistically "grown up" since his youthful attempt to be "the Jamaican Bobby Burns"; and, in the brief four years between *Banjo* and *Banana Bottom*, he had discovered a balance between art and message that he was never to realize again after the Jamaican novel. In fact, *Banana Bottom* was to be his last published novel; after it, one finds him turning increasingly to nonfictional prose forms, to autobiography and sociological treatises. The period of the writing of *Banana Bottom* almost seems, therefore, the first and last time in McKay's life that he felt comfortably assured of his unique creative genius and fully expressed it. Previously, during the days of his greatest fame—the "If We Must Die" period — he had not learned to match form with content. After his return to America from Morocco, McKay's world view and his sense of personal loyalties were to undergo profound and disturbing changes. However, in the early 1930s, McKay mentally returned home to his native island hills, rediscovered the materials for his masterpiece, and presented them in an artistic form that was uniquely his and precisely right. Obviously, he had been "a long way from home" for a long time; and the creation of *Banana Bottom* was the closest he ever came to returning.

Given McKay's addiction to adolescent male fantasy in *Home to Harlem* and in *Banjo*, it is pleasantly surprising that he focused his best novel on the character of a proud, independent woman, Bita

Plant. Bita represents all the intuitive black pride of a Jake or a Banjo, as well as considerable intellectual power; but the conflicts McKay sees as inherent in such a complex personality are resolved dramatically and believably. Bita is McKay's most successfully sustained characterization; and, when she chooses to merge intellect and instinct at the end of the novel, the reader feels that it is not only a possible choice but an inevitable one. As Bone points out, McKay, by discontinuing the use of Ray as his mouthpiece, ". . . achieved a proper distance between himself and his novel."[28] Moreover, by fusing Jake and/or Banjo and Ray into one character, he forced himself to dramatize the internal conflicts of that character. Then, when he made that character a woman, he demonstrated a sensitivity toward that sex of which, on the basis of *Home to Harlem* and *Banjo*, one might have believed him incapable.

Bita Plant's last name is significant. As will be shown, McKay makes effective use of the luxuriant and exotic flowers of Jamaica; and Bita is as much a natural product of the island as its giant ferns and its green bananas. But her education and, more importantly, her natural intelligence distinguish her from a simple earth-mother figure. Much of the novel, especially the last half, is concerned with Bita's coming to grips with her sexuality; but that is accomplished with no loss of intellectuality.

Stephen Bronz accurately describes the first half of the novel as "pastoral"; moreover, it has none of the stridency of *Banjo*.[29] There is a feeling of relaxation in the narration that one finds nowhere else in McKay, and Kenneth Ramchand understands the significance of this tranquility: McKay is leisurely establishing the folk community of Banana Bottom which possesses "spontaneous values of its own"; and his relaxed creation of that folk community provides a milieu for Bita's story that is essential to its artistic success.[30] McKay's achievement is impressive because he has attained a perfect union of narrative tone with content. The short exclamatory phrases of *Home to Harlem*, while appropriate to that novel, would be destructive to the creation of Bita's native village; therefore, one finds a prose in *Banana Bottom* that is as tranquil and as unhurried as life in the village. McKay's objective in the novel is to integrate the passion of Bita's sexual awakening *and her intellectuality* with that pastoral setting; and he accomplished that goal extremely well.

Moreover, there are indications from the beginning of the novel that Bita's struggle with her sexual self is to be the main theme of *Banana Bottom*. At the age of twelve, Bita is "raped" by the eccen-

tric village boy Crazy Bow. Actually, theirs was a spontaneous act of
sex not forced by either party; but, partly because of village-gossip
Sister Phibby Patroll and partly because of the respectable social
position of the Plant family, rape is what the village considers their
sex to have been. Crazy Bow is sent to an asylum; and Bita is taken
by a white missionary couple, Malcolm and Priscilla Craig, to be
reared in a proper — meaning white — manner. This episode indicates that Bita's sexuality is an intense part of her being, and it
foreshadows the ultimate failure of the Craigs to stifle it. For that is,
of course, what they attempt to do. As Bone points out, another early
hint of the Craigs' inevitable defeat comes when McKay indicates
that Sister Phibby Patroll, even while narrating to Priscilla Craig the
story of Bita's seduction, secretly considers it "a good thing done
early."³¹

The Craigs' plan for Bita is to give her a good education in
England and then, upon her return to the island as an enlightened
and proper young lady, have her marry a black youth who is training
to become a pastor. She would then be a living symbol to the
islanders of the power of Christian redemption — an effect only
heightened if anyone remembers the Crazy Bow incident (and
everyone assuredly would). Thus, from the first, Bita is a guinea pig
to the Craigs, a noble experiment, part of the white Christian's
burden. To them, she is never a person who might have needs and
desires of her own. McKay solidifies his central dualism with Bita's
adoption by the Craigs, who are his most complete personifications
of Western civilization. They are more effective for this symbolic
purpose than the Satanists of *Banjo* because they are less extreme,
closer to the norm.

Bita's seduction by Crazy Bow, her adoption by the Craigs, and
her education in England have all occurred before the novel opens
and are told in sequences of flashbacks. *Banana Bottom*'s first scene
describes Bita's return to the town of Jubilee, the locale of the Craig
mission, where she reenters the life of the island by playing
background piano to the singing of the "coloured choristers." It has
been seven years since she has visited home; for, while the Craigs encouraged her to visit the continent while receiving her education,
they did not wish her to return to Jamaica until she had become a
"lady." Herald Newton Day, the young man selected as Bita's future
husband, finds the arrangement totally satisfactory — he will
become a power in the village of Jubilee and gain an attractive,
enlightened wife in the process.

While the Craigs are totally confident of Herald, they are about the only people who see anything worthwhile in him. Bita and the reader form an aversion to him on first meeting, and it is immediately obvious that McKay's attitude toward the future missionary is one of utter contempt. Indeed, Herald is a repugnant combination of rampant egotism, false humility, and contempt for his fellow blacks. Perhaps the ultimate example in McKay of a black man who has lost touch with his race, Herald already thinks so like the whites that he does not even have to struggle to hide any innate black consciousness. His "courtship" of Bita consists primarily of singing the praises of himself, the Craigs, and Christ in about that order. When McKay disposes of Herald, he does so with a vengeance that somewhat bothers even his most sympathetic critics. Yet, as will be argued, Herald's fall from grace is thematically in keeping with the rest of the novel. The future missionary's name is an exercise in irony — to the Craigs, he is the herald of a new day; but neither the prophet nor the "age of salvation" is a success.

Obviously, the Craigs' plan for Bita is a monstrous thing: they cannot conceivably have her real welfare at heart when they envision her union with Herald. Unquestionably an implied comment about the Anglo-Saxon mind, the Craigs represent a white tendency to fasten mentally on a concept and to become so immersed in that concept that all considerations of other people and even of reality itself are discarded. They concentrate so intently on bringing the "heathen" to Christ that they are totally oblivious to the very human needs of their black charges. Also, they focus so completely on this one religious objective that they warp their own emotional and sexual beings. Herald is an example to them of the power in their own unnatural and repressed personalities to make monsters out of those in their control; and, with the very best of intentions, they intend to force Bita to marry this monstrosity. The Craigs are the most frightening white characters McKay ever created precisely because they are so well intentioned; the Satanists of *Banjo* at least recognize their own evil.

But what is perhaps even more disturbing than the inhumanity of the Craigs is the acquiescence of virtually everyone in Jubilee and Banana Bottom to their plans for Bita. Bita's father, Jordan Plant, a strong and admirable character, dares not object to anything the Craigs propose for Bita. What emerges then, and without a Ray to verbalize it, is McKay's thesis of the destructive effects of white civilization on natural black values. In fact, McKay does a masterful job of dramatizing the Craigs' human inadequacy. Priscilla Craig, especially, is a vivid example of a woman in warfare with her sexuality; and her main complaint about the blacks of Jamaica is that "they did not seem to grasp the meaning of the high social significance of existence. Sex was approached too easily" (16). Obviously, to her, sex, when it is acknowledged at all, is to be regarded as a necessary duty that is not to be discussed any more than possible. The Craigs have one child ". . . that could not talk and had developed into an adult without getting beyond the creeping state. The natives called him Patou, which was the dialect word for screech-owl, because he was subject to recurring crises when he would suddenly double up and make an eerie noise like a screech-owl" (27). Patou is a personification of Priscilla's attitude toward sex: something grotesque and humiliating.

The central conflict of the novel would appear quite clear. As Bone summarizes it, ". . . on the one side is the Christ God, the Calvinist austerity, and the naive ethnocentrism of the Mission. On the other is the Obeah God, the primitive sexuality, and the simple values of the folk culture."[32] But, as previously pointed out, McKay's content and intent are never quite that simple. Bita is, in fact, the best example in McKay's fiction of someone who finally rejects the corruption and perversion of the Anglo-Saxon world for the simple black life but who still retains what is of value in that white culture. She proves Kent's thesis that McKay's romanticism was never so complete that he advocated attempting to exist in the twentieth century in a totally primitive state. Bita personifies McKay's realization of something he should perhaps have always known — that one can combine the best aspects of Jake and Ray into a mature, integrated personality. Moreover, Christ is rejected in *Banana Bottom*, but the primitive god, Obeah, is scarcely advocated. Allegiance to Obeah and primitivism to the exclusion of intellect is represented by three other characters in the novel: Hopping Dick, Tack Tally, and Yoni Legge. While they are certainly more attractive than the Craigs, they are ultimately seen to be incomplete and to contrast with the full development Bita attains at the end of the novel. In fact, only Hopping Dick merits any detailed discussion.

Hopping Dick is an especially significant character for two reasons: his entry into the novel foreshadows the ultimate defeat of the Craigs' plans for making Bita into a respectable lady of the church; and, while he is, in many ways, reminscent of Jake and Banjo, he is still not the final answer for Bita. Bita transcends Hopping

Dick but not before having had a period of strong attraction to him. With "a reputation of being wild," Hopping Dick is "a dandy thing, a great and ever-welcome dancer and buyer of things at the tea-meetings, and fine-strutting in the peg-top clothes that were then the fashion" (39 - 40). The "tea-meetings," which are the natives' spontaneous and sensuous form of entertainment, are an effective symbol for Hopping Dick; and the source of his appeal to Bita is obvious: he personifies that aspect of herself which the Craigs are attempting to have her deny and which Herald Newton Day has *apparently* denied.

Yet Hopping Dick's ultimate inadequacy as a mate for Bita is obvious from the beginning, for he lacks even the level of seriousness of a Jake, and most certainly of a Bita. Priscilla Craig, however, almost causes Bita to marry Hopping Dick because Priscilla objects so harshly and so condescendingly every time she hears of a meeting between the two. Finally, Bita, realizing that she cannot and will not deny her sexuality and independence of spirit, agrees to marry the dandy "with a reputation of being wild" purely to demonstrate her independence from the Craigs. Ironically, the inadequacy of Hopping Dick's character is all that prevents the marriage.

McKay's description of the initial meeting between Bita and Hopping Dick is an excellent technical and stylistic achievement. Bita goes to the native market and instantly feels ". . . the sensation of a reservoir of familiar kindred humanity into which she had descended for baptism" (40). Significantly, she is intuitively aware that she would never have had that feeling of oneness with the black masses had she not been totally isolated from them for so long. The artistic superiority of *Banana Bottom* to *Banjo* is perhaps best illustrated by this incident: Ray tells the reader about his newly found kinship with the masses for almost two-hundred pages; McKay dramatizes the same awareness in Bita in one effective scene. At this precise moment when Bita is so intensely responding to blackness in others and in herself, Hopping Dick, the epitome of every aspect of the peasantry with which the church is at war, appears. He begins his courtship immediately, with an imitation-white gallantry that fails totally to hide his real self. Thus the battle for Bita's soul is joined: the Craigs, Christ, and duty on one hand; and Hopping Dick, black self-awareness, and sexual freedom on the other.

It is appropriate that a character whose name is laden with sexual connotation initiates Bita's sexual awakening. Hopping Dick's appearance at the market is the catalyst, but the hold of the Craigs and the sense of obligation in Bita are so strong that her struggle to attain a black identity is an extremely complex one. More and more, she feels an intense desire to attend a "tea-meeting," but her sense of restraint is at first too strong for her to overcome. McKay then achieves a fine technical effect by describing an elaborate church service immediately after Bita has fought back a particularly strong temptation to attend a "tea-meeting." That Bita's thoughts are on other things than Christ is made evident by an elaborate description of the wild Jamaican plants and flowers that decorate the church; throughout the novel, the Jamaican plant life connotes passion and sensuality. During the service, Bita notices that her father's eyes are dimmed with tears; and she remembers that her "rape" by Crazy Bow occurred immediately after she had received a Sunday School good conduct award. The native ditty that immortalized that long-ago event runs through her mind: "Crazy Bow was first,/Crazy Bow was first" (162).

Although it is inevitable that she will throw off the domination of the Craigs, the intervention of Squire Gensir is necessary before Bita attends her first "tea-meeting." Squire Gensir is an interesting character; but his presence in the novel seems elaborate and forced. McKay's "author's note" explains this awkwardness: "This story belongs to the Jamaican period of the early nineteen hundreds, and all the characters, as in my previous novels, are imaginary, excepting perhaps Squire Gensir." Gensir is obviously modeled closely on Walter Jekyll, Claude McKay's own white "sponsor" in Jamaica; and, once again, McKay's difficulty in handling characters based too closely on his actual background is apparent. Ray nearly always remains too abstract because he is, in large degree, McKay; Gensir seems not to be a character in a work of fiction, but an intruder in a novel, because he *is* McKay's first patron.

At any rate, Gensir, a freethinking exile from England who lives among the peasants collecting and writing down their songs and studying their dialects, takes an immediate interest in Bita. An effective opponent of the Craigs, he is able to assist Bita in acceptance of her blackness and of her self. Despite his reputation as a freethinker, he is a wealthy, titled white Englishman and thus not even the Craigs can criticize him directly. It is finally Gensir who persuades Bita to attend a "tea-meeting" with him, and she is able to accept because she will be in the company of such a respectable white man. Throughout most of the "tea-meeting," Bita maintains control over the temptation to join the entertainment and simply watches from a distance; finally, though, she abandons her self-restraint and joins in the dancing. Her dancing causes a sensation, and it is not long before Sister Phibby Patroll gets the word of the event to the Craigs. Bita has guessed correctly, however, because Priscilla Craig abandons her attack when she learns that Bita was escorted by Squire Gensir. An interval existed, however, between Priscilla's learning of Bita's performance at the "tea-meeting" and discovering that she was in safe, white hands. During that time, Priscilla begins to doubt for the first time the possibility of "saving" Bita and philosophizes that Bita and her race are "atavistic" (92 - 93).

Bita's dancing at the "tea-meeting" and her feeling of naturalness definitely aroused her sexuality; and, as a result, her life at the mission becomes increasingly tense. At this point, Bita is able to escape the mission for a weekend visit to her former home in Banana Bottom; and two events of significance happen during this visit. First, Bita really notices for the first time her father's drayman, Jubban; but it is a tribute to the subtlety of *Banana Bottom* that one is not to realize the full importance of Jubban for some time. Second, Bita decides to pay a sentimental return visit to her childhood swimming hole; what follows is one of the most effectively sensuous scenes McKay ever wrote. On arriving at the swimming hole, Bita observes five nude young boys in the water; her eyes search their bodies for pubic hair as she wonders ". . . how much more time it would take for them to be full-fledged men" (116). Then, retreating to a more secluded part of the pond, Bita strips and plunges into the water. For an indefinite "delicious" time, Bita floats, luxuriating in the touch of sun and water on every part of her body. Her act is a symbolic defiance of the Craigs' control, and it is perhaps more meaningful even than the dancing at the "tea-meeting." McKay ends the scene on a comic note: when she climbs out of the water, Bita discovers first that her clothes are missing and then that Tack Tally has been watching her the whole time, just as she had watched the five young boys. However, Tack Tally's appearance at the scene is not important; Bita's literal shedding of restraint is what matters.

The next climax in Bita's struggle to free herself comes at the Harvest Festival, a church-oriented celebration of the fertility of the Jamaican crops. The event brings together Hopping Dick and Herald Newton Day, and Bita perversely decides to introduce them. Herald acts so stiffly and condescendingly during the meeting between the two that Bita is unable to keep herself from laughing at him. Her open amusement at Herald's pomposity signals that he will not be able to hold her loyalty much longer.

Soon after Harvest Day, Bita is trapped into arranging a meeting between Herald and Squire Gensir. Once again, Herald is totally ridiculous: he again assumes his imitation-white superiority to the heathen. But he is sharply rebuffed by Bita: " 'I thank God that although I was brought up and educated among white people I have never wanted to be anything but myself. I take pride in being coloured and different, just as an intelligent white person does in being white . . .' " (169). This speech is important because it demonstrates Bita's awareness of what it took Ray two novels to learn — that no contradiction exists between being black and creatively intellectual. Gensir, who immediately realizes the superficiality of Herald, exploits it in conversations about "progress" and about the "debt of Blacks to Civilization" to the scarcely repressed delight of Bita. Finally, Gensir brings the subject around to music; and Herald praises classical white music and denounces black "popular" music. He ends his tirade with the remark that it is too bad the "serious music" is so often perverted by its use as an accompaniment to such a "degrading" pastime as dancing. This last comment is too much for Bita, and she changes the subject.

Obviously, Herald is almost too repulsive to be real; and McKay disposes of him before long in a startling manner: Herald sexually assaults a goat. For critics who dislike McKay, this episode is simply proof of the novelist's perverted atavism; and it troubles even the sympathetic ones like Ramchand. Yet the episode of Herald and the goat is thematically relevant. No one could be as devoid of sexual impulse and as inhumanly religious as Herald appears to be; because of the influence of the Craigs, he has attempted to deny all desire in himself. Because of such denial he has become something monstrous; and, when his unnatural and impossible restraint is shattered, he commits a monstrous act.

With Herald now out of the way, Hopping Dick is free to make his move. With instinctive shrewdness, he invites Bita to a dance; Bita knows that she is a "natural dancer" and the invitation is irresistible. Of course, the native dances are frowned upon by the fundamentalist white churches, but such dances are explained by McKay as being inevitable because the Negroes ". . . still possess more of primitive positiveness than formal hypocrisy . . ." (193). It is difficult for Bita to escape the mission without being detected by the Craigs, but ". . . her native prowess as a country wilding served her well and she [gets] away by climbing down a wild tamarind tree that grew stretching a strong limb over the veranda towards her room" (193). The phallic imagery in this escape scene is obvious. Needless to say, Bita has a splendid time with Hopping Dick at the dance.

While Bita is enjoying herself with Hopping Dick at the dance,
Priscilla Craig is visiting a missionary couple who have brought a
collection of primitive masks and idols from Africa. Throughout the
evening, Priscilla is unable to take her eyes off the pagan symbols;
and she ultimately falls under their hypnotic spell:

> But gazing again at the masks, they all seemed to be hideously grinning, and
> impelled to the wall by a magnetic power she attempted to touch one of
> them to test the reality of her eyes, when the mocking thing suddenly
> detached itself and began dancing around her. Others followed the first and
> Priscilla found herself surrounded by a grinning, dancing fury.
>
> Priscilla remained transfixed, deprived of voice to shriek her utter terror
> among those bodiless barbaric faces circling and darting towards her and
> bobbing up and down with that mad grinning. And now it seemed that
> Patou was among them, Patou shrunken to a grinning face, and suddenly
> she too was in motion and madly whirling round and round with the weird
> dancing masks (199).

Priscilla has almost realized her inner fear and hatred of blacks, of
her own sexual nature, and of the bond in her subconscious between
the two; and her near realization has terrified her. McKay, in an
effective dramatic passage, makes the point about white neurosis
regarding blacks and sex that is to be a major theme in subsequent
Afro-American fiction. That Patou has shrunken to a grinning mask
in Priscilla's hallucination is perhaps the most telling point in this
scene; Patou, the product of her sexual intercourse with Malcolm,
has always represented the grotesque and the unnatural to her; but
he is now equated with blackness. Priscilla, except for the duty of
gratifying Malcolm, never experiences fulfillment herself; and this
nightmarish experience results. Priscilla's own sexual and racial
neurosis played a critical role in the destruction of Herald. He was
her protégé, and she taught him to abhor his sexual needs and to see
them as monstrous.

Later that night, after Priscilla is in bed asleep, Bita returns from
the dance; and, "as Bita tiptoed in her stockings past Mr. Craig's
bedroom, Priscilla's eyes blinked open and she had a dim, unpleas-
ant, confused impression of a dark nymph and African masks and
Patou gyrating around her" (201). The next morning, when the
black maid Rosyanna is cleaning the Craigs' room, Priscilla rushes in
and grabs something out of the bed while she has momentarily distracted the maid and then proceeds to keep it elaborately out of
Rosyanna's sight. Rosyanna, knowing intuitively that it is some ap-
paratus relating to sexual intercourse, is outraged that Mrs. Craig

feels compelled to pretend to a black servant that she never has relations with her own husband. Obviously, Priscilla did her duty for Malcolm that night despite (or perhaps because of?) the experience with the African masks; but it is not surprising that she indeed would like her black inferiors to believe that she is still pure. Rosyanna, outraged at being treated like a child, recounts the story to Bita; and Bita, now fully realizing and enjoying her own sexuality, knows that her days at the mission are inevitably numbered.

To bring the situation to a head, Bita forces the Hopping Dick issue to a climax by insisting that she will marry him. Now facing the ruin of her "noble experiment," Priscilla Craig decides ". . . that Bita at bottom was a nymphomaniac" (221); and she sends an urgent message to the Plant home in Banana Bottom. Hopping Dick, confronted with the actual possibility of marrying Bita and of being financially responsible for her, quickly retreats. Even so, since no alternative to Bita's leaving the mission and returning to Banana Bottom exists, she breaks with the unnatural restraint with which she has tried to live; and, even though a suitable mate is not in sight, she is on her way to McKay's version of salvation. Priscilla Craig's reaction to Bita's "treachery" is predictable: she sees it as the final proof that her "great Work" has been hopeless from the start because one simply cannot save backward people.

The Craigs' control over Bita is now shattered, and Hopping Dick's irresponsibility has removed him as a factor in her life. Demonstrating McKay's growth since *Banjo* is the fact that Hopping Dick's refusal to accept the responsibility of marriage is fully in keeping with Banjo's final speech to Ray about the necessity of their not letting any woman tie them down. McKay, however, does not commend Hopping Dick's decision, as he did Banjo's.

After her break with the Craigs, Bita does have one moment in which she completely abandons intellect because of the spell of primitivism; but her experience with Obeah-like paganism serves as a purging effect for all her pent-up emotion and sexuality. During the period of the Christian revival that converts Hopping Dick and Yoni Legge, Squire Gensir proposes that he and Bita attend one of the evangelical meetings to enjoy the spectacle. Just at the moment that the revival meeting turns into an elaborate attempt to convert Squire Gensir, a black woman beating a drum and a group of men and women singing and carrying supplejacks enter the church. The congregation rushes outside, and a distinctly non-Christian religious celebration occurs; for one by one, members of the group groan and swoon, whereupon they are whipped with the supplejacks. Bita is enchanted by the scene; and, when the pull of her sensations is too much, she throws herself on the ground, ready to submit her body to the blows of the supplejacks.

There is obviously much significance to this scene: Bita is atavistically responding to the appeal of pagan tribal worship, and she is also debasing her sexuality in an attempt to attain masochistic gratification. Before Bita can be struck, she is rescued by Jubban; and the reader remembers that Jubban had once before soundly drubbed Tack Tally for telling a joke about Bita and Crazy Bow. This rescue makes it obvious where McKay is going: Jubban represents the best of the black peasantry; he is a very serious and much more than competent worker; and he is a strong, proud man. The fact that his station in life is merely that of the Plant family drayman has never diminished either his self-respect or his sense of self-worth. When one remembers McKay's own admiration of the black working class in America and Ray's thesis that true black art must come from the masses, he realizes the inevitability of a Bita-Jubban union.

To emphasize that Bita's giving herself to Jubban will not involve a denial of either pride or intellectuality, McKay adds an episode that, at first glance, seems out of place in and artificially imposed on the narrative. Bita is accosted by Arthur, the son of the wealthy renegade landowner Busha Glengley, while walking on the Glengley estate. There is one narrative weakness here: McKay tells just enough about the Glengley family background to get the reader intrigued, and then he abruptly promises to continue the account in *Gingertown*. But the basic facts are presented: Arthur is "near-white"; he represents wealth and power; and he is determined to have Bita sexually. Bita resists; Arthur contemptuously calls her " 'only a nigger gal' " (266); and he is fully intent upon raping her. Jubban appears, subdues Arthur, and knocks his white planter's hat (a symbol of the days of slavery) to the ground.

Later alone in her room, the taunt of "only a nigger gal" sticks in Bita's mind, and she is momentarily sickened by the universality of white prejudice. She goes to her mirror and undresses; she feels intense pride in her blackness and in her sexuality; and she opens a book and reads Blake's "The Little Black Boy" and realizes that, whatever the inadequacies of the poem, Blake and the great universal minds view racism as a brutal, ridiculous prejudice. Moreover, she knows that, married to Jubban or to anyone else, nothing prevents her from communion with those universal minds. Although George E. Kent objects to the union of Bita and Jubban as "unlikely" and as an escape on McKay's part from really facing the complex problems he has raised,[33] the marriage of Bita and Jubban and the description of Bita's reading Blake seem the best examples in McKay of Kent's own thesis that the Jamaican novelist advocated black pride and integrity but with the utilization of the best from Western civilization.

The major issues of the novel now virtually resolved, McKay rushes toward a conclusion. A hurricane and flood hit Jubilee and Banana Bottom while Malcolm Craig and Jordan Plant are away at a church conference; desperately attempting to return home in a horse-drawn coach, Malcolm, despite the advice of the coachman and Jordan, insists that they cross a swollen, rampaging river. The carriage is flooded immediately; Jordan scrambles out and attempts to save Craig; but the minister pulls them both to their death. The last thing the coachman, who survives, hears is Malcolm Craig calling, " 'Lord have mercy!' " "Thus Malcolm Craig went down to his death carrying Jordan Plant," writes McKay (284); and one could have no better symbol than death for the Craigs' effect on the blacks they meant to save.

Jubban and Bita go together to claim Jordan's body; and, on the way home, Jubban gives the mules their head; and he and Bita make love in the wagon carrying her father's body. After a proper interval, their marriage takes place, despite objections of the Reverend Lambert (a kind of modified Herald Newton Day); and Squire Gensir is Jubban's best man. At the village celebration afterward, Hopping Dick and his friends entertain themselves in their characteristic fashion until Jubban, who has permitted the celebration to continue as long as he thinks proper, quietly but firmly ends it. Then, in perhaps the most arbitrary segment of the novel, Squire Gensir returns to England, grows ill, dies, and leaves Bita his land and his home. McKay intrudes on the narrative with a lengthy tribute to the essential humanity of Gensir in comparison to all other whites, which is really a tribute to Walter Jekyll.

The novel ends with an idyllic scene involving Bita and her little son, Jordan. Bita is then seen reading Pascal, thinking how much greater a man he was ". . . than the Christian creed in which he was confined" (314). Thinking about the implications of Pascal's philosophy, Bita falls asleep, to be awakened by the sound of little Jordan playing in the yard outside. This ending is believable, while that of *Banjo* is not, precisely because one has seen Bita merge instinct with intellect. She has proved that she can be true to her black self without repudiating the humane white legacy of Blake and Pascal, as well as all the great Western minds who transcended racism. She has committed herself to the masses with no loss in her ability to respond to art. Indeed, it is but a short step from that point to joining the masses and, through their inspiration, creating art. Since Bita rejoins her native village from which she has been arbitrarily separated, her union with Jubban is relevant to McKay's faith in community solidarity as the best means of black progress.

More must be said about the symbolic significance of Crazy Bow. Ramchand's analysis of him is interesting; he writes that Crazy Bow represents essentially the same values as Banjo but that, while those values must not be ignored, the world of *Banana Bottom* is so "well-proportioned" that there is no need for Crazy Bow to be a "central" character.[34] There is undeniably some merit to this argument, for both Banjo and Crazy Bow possess an "instinctive" gift for music; they both refuse utterly to bow to the conventions of white society; and they suffer in differing degrees for their refusal to conform. It is probably this last point that is significant; for although Crazy Bow never raped anybody, he was still declared insane and put away by the white power structure. Significantly, he makes one last appearance in the novel. During the period of the big "Revival," he suddenly appears in the schoolroom where Bita and the teacher Fearon, a musician himself, are playing. Crazy Bow simply walks past Bita, gives her no sign of recognition, but takes her place at the organ and begins to perform. He goes from the oratorio of Judas Maccabaeus to spirituals like "Swing Low, Sweet Chariot" to "tea-meeting" songs and jigs and even quadrilles. A crowd instantly assembles. Significantly, the brilliance of Crazy Bow's performance is what shatters the spell of the great "Revival."

This represents his one moment of triumph, his short-lived revenge over the forces that have destroyed him; for, whatever his original mental condition, Crazy Bow is soon to be destroyed. Shortly after his moment of victory in the schoolroom, he goes to the mission and attempts to strangle Patou. This episode implies a bitter irony: Crazy Bow's strangling of Patou represents a symbolic counterattack against the very symbol of that grotesque perversion that is inherent in the white power structure that wrought the destruction of Crazy Bow. The musician probably does not realize the symbolic meaning of his attack on the retarded child of Priscilla

Craig, but McKay does. Perhaps McKay might be vulnerable to the charge of bad taste in making a retarded child the victim of Crazy Bow's attack; but one must remember that it is Priscilla Craig who most strongly regards Patou and the sexual act that created him as being grotesque, and it is Priscilla Craig who set in motion the incarceration of Crazy Bow. It might be added that McKay does not want the reader to forget that, if Arthur Glengley had succeeded in raping Bita, absolutely nothing would have been done to punish him.

Real anger exists beneath the calm surface of *Banana Bottom*, but the novel is the successful culmination of a search for a proper wedding of form and content that began with a novel set in Harlem and then continued with one set in Europe; both books incorporated characters from every segment of the black world. Indeed, McKay is making, in part, a comment about the vicious racism of America and Europe when he is only able to write an acceptable happy ending for a novel set in a rural Jamaica that he had not seen for some years. However, all three novels are, for the same reason, vital to any study of Afro-American, Pan-African, or West Indian literature because of their stress on the necessity not only of attaining a defiant black pride and black consciousness through identification with the masses, but also of taking from the white world what it has of value to offer. The revolutionary nature of that thesis, especially in Afro-American literature, is difficult to exaggerate. That there are serious artistic flaws in *Home to Harlem* and especially in *Banjo* does not destroy the significance of this concept. McKay's stress in his novels about the importance of remaining faithful to one's blackness in spite of whatever pressures or enticements the white world offered was light years ahead of the Chesnutt-Dunbar school. In McKay's absolute refusal to admit the necessity, or even validity, of any external "uplifting" of the masses in his novels, he went far beyond the spirit of the Harlem Renaissance. This last point is precisely why McKay has so often been condemned as a traitor to the Renaissance. Artistic pioneers usually are condemned, especially when they are as individualistic as was Claude McKay.

CHAPTER 4

Gingertown: *Studies of Self-hatred*

PUBLISHED in 1932 after *Home to Harlem* and *Banjo* and before *Banana Bottom*, McKay's collection of twelve stories, *Gingertown*, nicely complemented his three novels. The first six stories in the volume — "Brownskin Blues," "The Prince of Porto Rico," "Mattie and Her Sweetman," "Near-White," "Highball," and "Truant" — are Harlem stories with particular emphasis upon the social and psychological overtones of skin coloring; and, in style and somewhat in content, they resemble *Home to Harlem*. Jamaica is the setting for the next four stories, "The Agricultural Show," "Crazy Mary," "When I Pounded the Pavement," and "The Strange Burial of Sue." As in *Banana Bottom*, McKay celebrates native simplicity and "black passion" and attacks the corrupting influences of the Christian church and the colonial governmental bureaucracy. A city like Marseilles is the locale for "Nigger Lover"; and the story, which revolves around a prostitute with an international clientele in an "extensive and lively [Mediterranean] Southern port,"[1] could easily have been incorporated into *Banjo*. The final story, "Little Sheik," set in North Africa, has the same international flavor as Banjo's and Ray's story.

The twelve stories reveal McKay to be uneven in his mastery of the technique of the short story. For instance, "Truant," which has been anthologized in John Henrik Clarke's *American Negro Short Stories*, is essentially a character sketch of a West Indian black who has adopted the United States and New York, who has gotten married, and who has found regular, respectable life in the American metropolis to be unbearably limiting. Preparing at the end to desert wife, child, and job, he decides that his existence must be one of "eternal inquietude" (162). One almost feels that it is a thinly disguised piece of authorial self-examination rather than a short story. "The Agricultural Show" is an overly long loving tribute to

Jamaican folk customs, although it does contain valuable detail about Busha Glengley and his rise to landowner status, which supplements the limited information in *Banana Bottom*. "When I Pounded the Pavement" is essentially a satire of church and state interference with black loving; "Nigger Lover" is an interesting character sketch without sufficient incident to be called a story; and even "Brownskin Blues," which has the ingredients of a fine psychological study of black self-hatred, is marred by a sentimental ending. Yet "Mattie and Her Sweetman," "Near-White," "Highball," "Crazy Mary," and "The Strange Burial of Sue" are successful stories that are immeasurably strengthened, as always in McKay's best writing, by the flavor of setting.

I   The Harlem Stories

The most interesting stories are the ones about Harlem because they have *Home to Harlem*'s combination of the exotic and the desperate. Snatches of popular song, erotic dances, "parlor socials," and the sexual liaisons of "grass widows," real and pretended, produce the tone which DuBois found so offensive in McKay's first novel. Black, brown, and yellow skins determine both the social success and the psychological makeup of individual characters. The first five of the Harlem stories demonstrate that what Malcolm X called the "brainwashing" of blacks by white society results in racial self-hatred. Often, the beehive of Harlem provides an ironic twenty-four-hour-a-day backdrop of exhilaration to compensate for psychological suffering.

McKay introduces "Brownskin Blues" with his poem, "The Harlem Dancer." The theme of the exploitation of the black woman, which is so central to this poem, is also relevant to Bess, the heroine of "Brownskin Blues." A cabaret entertainer whose specialty is "the Wicked Wiggle," Bess trades the promise of her body for the applause and the scattered coins hurled at her by the nightclub habitués. Yet, Bess is even more seriously exploited by her own feelings about her skin color. Dark, she feels that she is obviously less desirable than a light-skinned girl. Moreover, she distrusts all light-skinned men because years ago her mulatto husband "jest left me lonely and misahable with mahself to go with a yaller hussy . . ." (11). However, her current black lover, Rascoe, has dropped her for another yellow-skinned rival; but Bess refuses to let Rascoe go because his blackness makes her — irrationally — feel safe.

Bess represents one of McKay's most skillful portrayals of a character chaotically driven by hatred of her own skin color. Rascoe is not only demonstrably unfaithful to her (early in the story he humiliates her by bringing Bess' yellow rival to the cabaret to watch the dark-skinned woman perform); he is hardly capable of fidelity to anyone or anything. Yet, since he is dark, he must be the man for a dark girl like Bess. Besides, she has long ago convinced herself that any light-skinned man would leave her permanently for a "yaller hussy"; and, being shunned again, this time by a quite worthless, quite black lover, may appeal to a capacity for self-abasement that is certainly present in Bess.

In desperation, Bess begs Rascoe to take her back; and, after he rejects her and calls her "a black sow" (17), she turns to skin bleaches in a pathetic attempt to destroy that blackness which she feels has always made her the victim. But the bleaches do not work; and, finally, in one of the best written scenes in McKay, Bess concocts a mixture of several bleaching lotions and salves and covers her face with it. Because the pain of the mixture on her face is so intense, Bess has to resort to cocaine; and an impressionistic dream sequence results:

> The cabaret was a vast hall, dazzlingly lit up. She was dancing upon a golden table. Barefooted, half naked. Coral beads around her throat and small red plates on her breasts and red bangles on her arms, and round her waist a short hooped thing of golden gauze. Black and white admirers threw money at her feet until the floor was green with dollars. She made a magnificent green mountain. She danced that red "Wicked Wiggle." The piano was a green elephant with the player on his back. And a great green moon swam round and round Bess, with the grinning drummer sitting on its rim and tapping it with two red sticks. And suddenly an immense jungle sprang up, of giant trees and vines like ropes, golden fruit and leaves all red. . . A mighty red jungle of blazing trees. Burning, blazing until they were reduced to a mass of strange flowers with red lips and fiery tongues singing all together a blues. . . blues . . . blues . . . blues . . . brownskin blues. (23)

The use of green and red is an impressive symbolic device: the green connotes both the money thrown at Bess' feet in the cabaret and the green jungle of her ancestral homeland where gradations of skin color would never have resulted in such psychological crippling; the red evokes the passion exemplified in Bess' "Wicked Wiggle" and the bleaching lotions presently burning her face.

When Bess awakens in a hospital, she is scarred for life because of her attempt to lighten away the blackness that she felt had made her undesirable even to a dark-skinned man like Rascoe. Ironically, one of her first questions to the doctor is, " 'But will it be mah own nacheral dark skin, smooth and clean as it use to be?' " (24) Until this point in the story, McKay has painted a memorable portrait of the "brainwashing" of a black girl.

Regrettably, however, McKay dissipates much of the effectiveness of "Brownskin Blues" with a trite and sentimental ending. Her face now scarred, Bess' career as a cabaret entertainer is ended; she is reduced to life as a scrubwoman. But Jack Newell, the one light-skinned man who has been consistently faithful to her, seeks her and vows that his love is unchanged despite the damage to her face. He even convinces her that her fixations about the relationship between skin color and fidelity are meaningless: " 'It ain't the color that counts, honey; it's the stuff. Every man his own stuff . . .' " (31). Bess is redeemed, therefore, by the love of a good man.

Despite the ending, "Brownskin Blues" is a fascinating early study in Afro-American writing of the curious social and psychological implications of skin coloring. It is not a far journey from Bess' pouring a foaming mixture of bleaching lotions on her face to Malcolm X's sticking his head in the toilet to remove burning lye from his hair.

"The Prince of Porto Rico," which ends with a murder, is nonetheless a more light-hearted story than "Brownskin Blues." The central character, who either owns or manages a barber shop, is a handsome Puerto Rican who personifies McKay's ideal of the sexually promiscuous male. He likes to love; he likes for no strings to be attached; and, so long as his women understand and accept this arrangement, he sees nothing wrong with it. Plenty of women do accept it, for the Prince, as he is called, is an attractive man.

The Prince's undoing comes when he meets Tillie Worms, "a pretty child, squat, plump, with the sweetest and softest maroon complexion." Tillie regularly attends Bella Rowan's buffet flat and pretends to be a grass widow while, in truth, her husband Uriah works nights. At Bella's, Tillie meets Hank Forbes and begins a liaison with him which lasts until the Prince enters. The Puerto Rican's attractiveness reduces Hank to "a repulsive black beast" (37) and "a great big black shiny and slimy snake" (40) in Tillie's eyes; and the Prince has the field to himself. Moreover, he can see no possible difficulties in his new arrangement with Tillie — he really believes that she is a grass widow and that he will have no trouble from Hank: " 'I can't imagine a man following a woman around when she's turned him down' " (41). But Hank does not surrender

Tillie so easily; for when he knows that Tillie and the Prince are at the ostensible grass widow's home, he informs the husband who rushes home and shoots the Puerto Rican. To add additional insult to the husband's injury, the Prince is, at the time, wearing Uriah's pajamas.

The story is a rather impressive attempt at conveying a tragicomic impression of Harlem's eroticism. McKay introduces the action with a description of Harlem's Saturday night ritual of the massage ("Sugar-brown experts bending over chocolate lads, luxuriating under the process and dreaming sweet-scented rendezvous with the chippies" [33]). Buffet flats serve the same function as they do in *Home to Harlem*: "To encourage and promote intrigues is the prime business of the keeper of a buffet flat. Successful intrigues bring good business and new customers" (36 - 37). But the figure of the Prince, the proponent of love which is sensual, enjoyable, and without binding commitment, gives the story its tone. His death in an alley in another man's pajamas prevents the reader from viewing him as more than he is; but what he is, to McKay, is not inconsiderable. Within his code, he is a man of complete honor who also happens to bring enjoyment to women who do not find it elsewhere. He is what every Harlem woman dreams of — a spiritually free man unmarked by the values of white Christian America. The Prince obviously is the embodiment of the "pagan" male venerated by the McKay of this period.

While the action and denouement of "The Prince of Porto Rico" are too slight for the story to be viewed as a really impressive achievement, it is an interesting minor addition to the McKay canon. One should emphasize too that skin color plays a part in its plot as well as in "Brownskin Blues." Tillie sees nothing wrong with Hank's blackness until the lighter-skinned Prince appears, and then her first lover becomes an object of repulsion. Like Bess, though in a less self-destructive way, Tillie is brainwashed by the white society. It is possible that McKay is having some ironic fun with the name, Tillie Worms, as with several names in *Gingertown*.

The degree of self-hatred which America can produce in a dark-skinned person is also the subject of "Mattie and Her Sweetman." Now in her fifties, Mattie is a very black woman with an abnormally long neck; she has been taught from youth that she is extremely ugly and she believes she is. When the story opens, Mattie is reduced to keeping Jay, an indigent "sweetman" who abuses her in public but who does, for a price, take her to parlor socials. Finally, at one such gathering, Jay refuses to dance with Mattie and refers to her loudly as "black woman." Mattie leaves, taking with her the overcoat she has bought for Jay; and, while waiting for Jay to come home, she broods over the "black woman" insult and remembers that, when she first came north and had been attracted to "a yellow man," he had laughed at her and called her a "black giraffe." That man long ago and Jay merge in her mind; and, when her "sweetman" does come home, he has his clothes thrown at him on the street and is told to "take a walk."

The characterization of Mattie makes this story one of the richest in the volume. Like Bess, she has allowed her skin color to make her a victim; self-hatred has been a motivating factor of her life. But Mattie has a "quiet, dark determination" (56) and "a smoldering fire in her ugly black body" (59 - 60); and there are limits to her capacity for self-humiliation, even without the support of a good man: "Years ago she had had a baby for a white man in South Carolina. But being one black woman who did not feel proud having a yellow pickaninny at any price, she had got rid of the thing, strangling it at birth and, quitting relatives and prayer-meeting sisters, made her way up North" (60). Beneath her self-contempt and her culturally imposed sense of inferiority, Mattie has pride that can erupt in sudden, even violent, action. One cannot imagine her scarring her face with a desperately concocted mixture of skin lighteners, for she permits being victimized only so far. Obviously, Mattie represents more of McKay's hope for the future of the race than does the performer of the "Wicked Wiggle."

In "Near-White," McKay turns his attention to the problems of the Negro of extremely light skin; in fact, he utilizes the "passing" theme which is the basis of such Afro-American novels as Chesnutt's *House Behind the Cedars*, James Weldon Johnson's *Autobiography of an Ex-Colored Man*, and Nella Larsen's *Passing*. In contrast to Chesnutt and Larsen, McKay avoids the excesses of the "tragic mulatto" motif; and he clearly does not regard the position of the story's central character, Angie Dove, as tragic. Light-skinned Angie's problem is essentially that she has simultaneously developed a loathing for Harlem, which she feels is suffocating her, and discovered the ease with which she can pass into white society. McKay introduces the story by describing the dance craze "The Butterfly," which has swept Harlem literally off its feet; and this dance becomes the recurring symbol of what Angie considers the frivolity of Harlem. But Angie's own dissatisfaction is what McKay views as frivolous. She is perfectly contented with being the unquestioned belle of Harlem until she meets Eugene Vincent who teaches her the technique of "passing." When Vincent disappears, Angie is thrown back into the "butterfly" world of Harlem; and, in McKay's words, "a pretty, irresponsible girl" becomes a "very discontented woman" (81).

But Angie, who refuses to be "discontented" long, is soon drawn back to the white world; at a theater, she meets a charming white man who is instantly enchanted by her. Two typical aspects of the "passing" theme then emerge: the lovers must have their rendezvous without his learning enough about her to discover her drop of black blood, and she must draw some declaration from him that he will love her no matter what. The potential ironies of such a situation are not missed by McKay, any more than they are by Chesnutt, Johnson, and Larsen; when Angie's white lover tells her that he would love her if she were Chinese (100), he also asserts that she is "the nicest, whitest little girl in the world for me" (99). The obligatory tragic climax comes when the two see a black man and a white girl together, and Angie's lover delivers a racist harangue. To Angie's subsequent question of whether he could love an octoroon or not, he exclaims, " 'Me! I'd sooner love a toad ' " (102). This admission ends Angie's vision of entrance into the white world.

The story is saved from triteness by McKay's skillful characterization of Angie. She is shallow; and the reader, knowing that, can hardly consider the end of her dream as very tragic. In a significant conversation with her mother, Angie argues that light-skinned Negroes like herself should go out of their way to love whites; but her mother, after describing all the humiliations which her family has received from white people especially during the Reconstruction period, asserts that " '. . . we belong to the colored race. Our feelings and our ties are colored. We will find more contentment being ourseves than in trying to climb in among the lily-whites who've done us all sorts of dirt' " (96). Angie's mother personifies the black pride which McKay consistently advocated; and her warning to her daughter that degrading submission to one's oppressors can only lead to a loss of identity strikes a contemporary note.

The only reason that Claude McKay would call Angie Dove a "tragic mulatto" is that she does not know who she is and is on the verge of "selling her birthright for a mess of pottage" (94) — a phrase also quoted in the ending of Johnson's *Autobiography of an Ex-Colored Man*.

"Highball," the most subtly developed story in the volume, is an account of Nation Roe, a successful black entertainer who is accepted into the world of white artists and performers but who never believes that his acceptance is complete. When Nation begins his career, he is happily married to a quite domestic black woman; but, as his popularity grows, he begins to long for a "brilliant-talking wife like one of the white actresses" (111). Discarding his first wife, Nation marries Myra Peck; and his troubles begin. (Nation's name may also have symbolic overtones: his music has its roots in the "nation" of black consciousness.)

In Myra, Nation gets a self-pitying, intellectually and emotionally shallow woman who uses her whiteness as a means of humiliating Nation. Since all of his white friends recognize Myra's petty viciousness, they consistently do not invite her to the parties to which Nation is welcome; and Myra easily convinces her husband that her exclusion is a slap at Nation for marrying a white woman. After Nation has finally assailed his theatrical associates for the racism implied in their treatment of Myra, he returns home to overhear Myra and her associates laughing about the "good old prune" (136) who keeps her so comfortably; and his world is totally shattered.

Myra is one of McKay's most skillful characterizations. Her knowledge that her color enables her to dominate Nation so ruthlessly is related to a strong but subtly developed implication of lesbianism. Myra has a friend named Dinah of whom she is particularly fond; and Dinah is just as fond about belittling Nation. The story skillfully depicts the vulnerability of the black man in America; Nation has been taught to desire a white woman, even a sick, man-hating one like Myra; and her sickness corresponds to her power over him. Myra is a product of that America which teaches that black men are not men, except sometimes as sexual brutes; and her lesbianism constitutes a shield against Nation's sexuality. Moreover, her ability to convince Nation so easily that his white friends resent his having married a white woman is evidence not only of her talent for psychological warfare but of his susceptibility to any charge of racism. Because of the color of his skin, Nation is as much a victim as Bess and Mattie.

An interesting stylistic device is employed in "Highball," as well as in "Brownskin Blues," "Mattie and Her Sweetman," and "Near-White"; for McKay builds potential conflicts and then has them explode through one spoken word or phrase. Bess is driven to self-mutilation by Rascoe's calling her a "black sow"; Mattie lets Jay go when he calls her "black"; Angie Dove's dreams of entering the white world are shattered when she is by implication referred to as a "toad"; and Nation's final humiliation comes when he overhears Myra's friends ridiculing him as a "prune." This device is associated with McKay's theme of the vulnerability of the black psyche in America; one word can trigger such overwhelmingly strong culturally induced feelings of inferiority and self-contempt that a life can shatter (or, as in the rare cases of the Matties, regenerate).

The final Harlem story, "Truant," serves as an effective transition into the four Jamaican stories. As mentioned, it is about a West Indian who adopts New York for a time; and it is more interesting for what it reveals about McKay than as a story. That note, found so often in the poems, of conflicting attraction to the calm, green naturalness of the West Indies and to the man-made steel and power of New York City is central to "Truant." Barclay Oram, the hero of the story, works for the railroad, is married to a woman he met at an American university, and has a child. His wife, Rhoda, is content with their black middle-class life; but Barclay is growing less so — he resents being a "boy" to the white people he serves on the trains, and he feels trapped in a meaningless life. The university had once symbolized the potentialities of intellectual power to Barclay, but he was seduced from that dream by Rhoda, especially by her mouth: "And her mouth: the full form of it, its strength and beauty, its almost unbearable sweetness, magnetic drawing, sensuous, exquisite, a dark pagan piece of pleasure . . ." (158). Now, years later, Rhoda's mouth is always full of chewing gum.

Barclay debates with himself: "the Moral Law" of this steel-and-stone civilization which he partially admires tells him that he cannot desert his wife and his child; but Barclay decides that, in this respect, "the grim frock-coated gentleman . . . that held humanity in fear" is not his god (160 - 161). His allegiance is to "other gods of strange barbaric glory" (160). So, in a decision strongly reminiscent of Ray's final choice in *Banjo*, he leaves and accepts "eternal inquietude."

II *The Jamaican Stories*

Of the four Jamaican stories, two, "Crazy Mary" and "The Strange Burial of Sue," are successful fiction. As mentioned, "The Agricultural Show" is essentially a sketch that depicts a folk celebration; while "When I Pounded the Pavement," a potent satire of imperial bureaucracy and its interference with native folkways, really lacks any fully developed plot or characterization. "The Agricultural Show" does contain relevant information, omitted from *Banana Bottom*, about the rogue imperialist, Busha Glengley, and his rise to landowner status. After beginning with nothing, Busha virtually owns Gingertown; his rise to power began with his liaison with a quadroon woman, the Widow Clavale, a former barmaid, who inherited property from her husband; and Busha has parlayed her inheritance into a vast estate. He has also populated the surrounding countryside with unknown numbers of illegitimate racially mixed children. Moreover, because of their own illegitimacy and drop of black blood, the children of Busha and the Widow Clavale, while wealthy, are denied real "respectability." The central theme of "The Agricultural Show" is their struggle to attain such "respectability."

"When I Pounded the Pavement" reflects the native Jamaican's dislike of the police, an arm of white imperialism. The story centers around two factors: first, the native narrator's brief experience as a colonial policeman and the pressure put on him in that capacity to "make a case" (arrest and convict some native black); second, a law, inspired by the Christian church and advocated even by its black ministers, to make it a crime for a black man to sleep with one of the black servant girls while she is living on her white employer's property. The penalty for this crime is imprisonment and flogging across the buttocks with a tamarind switch. The attitude exhibited by church and state is that the black Jamaican is not a man but a child who is to be treated as such; that this attitude is enforced by blacks does not disguise its white imperialist source.

The particular "crime" treated in the narrative illustrates McKay's central theme of the war which a mechanical and omnipresent white society has declared upon "black passion" as well as white imperialism's use of the Christian church as one of its main weapons in that war. The story ends when the narrator, much against his will, is trapped into "making his case" against a prominent young black man who has a promising political future. The young black is arrested, imprisoned, and humiliated with the switch; his future is destroyed; and the narrator leaves the police force. McKay's anger at the brutality, hypocrisy, and sterility of white imperialism is eloquently expressed but the story lacks adequate plotting and characterization.

"Crazy Mary," in contrast, is a nicely compact story of the psychological destruction of "a pretty young yellow woman" by the sexual hysteria of her village and by her own sexual repression. In *A Long Way From Home*, McKay declares that D. H. Lawrence is "the modern writer I preferred above any";[2] and one can see Lawrence's influence here. Mary's life begins with promise: she is pretty, her parents have prepared her for the position of village sewing-mistress, and everyone is confident that she will marry the young schoolmaster. Then one of her sewing students accuses the schoolmaster of molesting her; the village is in hysterics; and Mary, who attempts to defend the schoolmaster, is accused in public of corrupting the girl and of being the schoolmaster's mistress. When someone finally thinks of having the young girl examined by a doctor, the schoolmaster has disappeared. From that point on Mary becomes the local eccentric; she goes about barefoot, carrying bunches of flowers (one thinks of McKay's use of flowers as symbols of sexual passion in *Banana Bottom*). Mary, in fact, holds the bouquet she is perpetually carrying "as if she were nursing it" (200). She talks only to herself and answers questions "with a cracked little laugh"(200). Obviously, Mary's intense sexuality, repressed because of the scandal over the schoolmaster, is driving her mad.

Years later, when the schoolmaster returns with his wife to the village, the old scandal has been temporarily forgotten. In fact, he and his wife are celebrities at the Sunday church service; but after the service (in the churchyard), as the schoolmaster and his wife stand surrounded by old and new admirers, Mary appears. She tosses her bouquet at her one-time fiance; runs up the church steps; and exposes herself to the entire crowd, "looking at them from under with a lecherous laugh" (201). Running madly toward the graveyard, she repeats her exposure. The villagers attempt to catch the crazed woman for her own protection; but Mary, keeping at a safe distance from them, repeats her act of self-humiliation. Finally, in conduct reminiscent of Ophelia, Mary comes to a waterfall over the river and "on the perilous edge of the waterfall she halted and did her stuff again, then with a high laugh she went sheer over" (202).

Mary's tragedy is a result of her enforced repression of a strong sexuality. Bad luck and her own position as a "respectable" girl in the village society lead to her repression. Her final gesture is perhaps not so insane — it expresses her contempt not only for those villagers whose hysteria over the patently false charges of an adolescent girl ruined her life but also for the man who deserted her during that hysteria. That she had carried the visible symbol of her sexual need in those bouquets of flowers for years and that no one had noticed intensify her tragic isolation.

In "The Strange Burial of Sue," McKay presents the other side of

the coin — a woman with no pretensions to respectability and with
no restraints on her sexual appetite. Among the villagers, Sue lives
and dies as a loved, almost venerated, figure. In fact, to the peasants
Sue is known as "a good woman" "which means she was kind"
(223). She is the favorite nurse of anyone who happens to be sick,
and she is consistently generous with all she has. She is also completely free with her sexual appetites; when she becomes pregnant
by Sam Bryan while nursing his sick wife, no one, including Mrs.
Bryan, is upset. Sue marries a man named Nat Turner, but she does
not let her marriage interfere with her promiscuity; and Turner, like
almost everyone else, understands and accepts. Thus, Sue is a personification of McKay's ideal of "black passion."

The one person who refuses to accept Sue for what she is is a man
named Burskin, a slow-witted farm laborer whom Sue seduces in a
cane field. The seduction grows from a mock struggle over a piece of
cane, and meant everything to Burskin. In contrast, to Sue, it meant
only a momentary sexual fulfillment. When a man named Johnny
Cross appears on the scene, Sue loses interest in Burskin. McKay
again utilizes phallic symbolism in depicting the beginning of the
liaison between Sue and Johnny Cross; the two are celebrating at a
dance: "She was a strong wild dancer, and she flashed some bold
movements as they jig-a-jigged around the stout bamboo pole in the
center of the barbecue supporting the palm booth . . ." (234). Sue
attempts to dismiss Burskin; but the laborer refuses to let her go, and
he is finally reduced to vilifying her in the local tavern. When Sue
hears of Burskin's verbal abuse, she enters the tavern and physically
attacks him. Burskin's humiliation is increased by a ridiculous
countersuit between himself (he sues Sue for assault) and Nat Turner
(he sues Burskin for seducing his wife).

When the whole Burskin incident makes Sue the focus of village
gossip, the church enters the situation. The minister of Sue's church,
a "young brown graduate of the Baptist college" (237 - 38), reads
Sue out of church membership. Sue is so hurt by the entire affair that
she attempts to relieve her mental and spiritual pain by doing in-
human amounts of physical labor; and, in doing so, she kills herself.
As she is dying, the entire village comes to offer advice and consola-
tion; and her moment of death represents her triumph over the
forces of bigotry that have destroyed her: "Around midnight Sue
beckoned Turner to the bed and tried to embrace him. The women
laughed and cried 'Shame!' at Sue and Sue made a wry grin and died
in the midst of the laughter" (242). At that moment, in the eyes of

the village, Sue is again simply the generous, sensuous woman they love.

But the church does not alter its objective. At Sue's burial, the minister demands that solemn hymns like "Blacksliders, Repent" be sung; he chooses as text "The Barren Fig Tree"; and he then proclaims loudly that " 'Sue Turner is gone to hell.' " At this moment, Burskin shouts that, if Sue is in hell, he will go there too; and he has to be restrained from throwing himself into the open grave. Finally, Nat Turner pushes aside the minister and conducts his own service; and his text is "I am the resurrection and the life." Instead of preaching, he asks anyone who has anything to say against Sue to do so; but no one does. When he asks to hear from those who wish to say something in Sue's favor, many do so.

Turner and Burskin then stand together as the coffin is lowered into the grave; and, as the earth covers it, Turner says, " 'Lord, letteth now thy servant depart in peace' " (244 - 46). Sue is the servant of those gods which McKay felt Christian imperialism was destroying — the gods of pagan beauty which Barclay Oram of "Truant" chose to follow. Sue is indeed a saint of kindness and of physical pleasure. Her deification comes from the people (Nat, Burskin, all those who speak at her burial); but it would never come from the church.

But the source of Nat's final words is the Christian religion; and, perhaps, McKay means that what Sue personified (kindness and simple enjoyment of her total self) *is* in keeping with the original spirit of the Christian faith before it solidified into the institution of the church and before that church wedded itself to Western imperialism. McKay may also be saying that the simple pagan gods of Jamaica have more in common with that Eastern movement begun by a common carpenter than do most twentieth-century Christian churches. Finally, in contrast to Crazy Mary, who restrained her sexuality in the name of "respectability," Sue dies amidst love and laughter.

III   *"Nigger Lover"* and *"Little Sheik"*

The last two stories in the volume, "Nigger Lover" and "Little Sheik," represent a decline in the quality of "Crazy Mary" and "The Strange Burial of Sue." Just as "The Agricultural Show" seems like an omission of material once intended for *Banana Bottom*, "Nigger Lover" could well have have been included in *Banjo*, since it is only a sketch of a white prostitute in a Southern Mediterranean port who prefers black men as clients. This preference has earned her the nickname of "Nigger Lover," a sobriquet which is not meant unkindly. Nigger Lover's devotion to black lovers has nothing to do with any assumption of superior Negro virility, but arises from one instance in which a black client was especially kind to her. Instead of cheating her as he easily could have, he paid her far more than the expected price. Moreover, the Negro's act was unrelated to any outstanding professional attributes of the girl; it was simply an act of generosity. The central weakness of the story is that McKay really makes no effort to characterize Nigger Lover. Although he makes the same point he made in *Banjo* that all the girls of her profession long for some miraculous escape into respectability, he only describes her fondness for playing the piano and singing.

While not a successful story, "Little Sheik" contains more subtlety of theme and technique than "Nigger Lover." Set in North Africa, it contains rhapsodic passages about the mystery and enchantment of that land; but it is essentially another attack on Western imperialism — one that has more restraint than is typical of McKay. The catalyst of the story is "one of those [white] independent U. S. A. girls a little difficult of placing, socially or financially, who may run about in a coupe and know all kinds of persons and all sorts of things old and new" (260). This rather mindless young white woman wanders among the North Africans with a true sense of Yankee imperviousness; she sees a handsome young man and recruits him for a guide. To her he is a "little sheik" — a phrase that implies a curious combination of condescension and sexual excitement; for the girl is mentally teasing herself with visions of being seduced by a Valentino-like barbarian.

The young man takes her virtually everywhere, even to the university, forbidden to women. There he even shows her one of the student's studios. At the studio, the student sends the "little sheik" to buy some cakes; and he then offers her the exotic sexual fulfillment which she has been titillating herself with all day. She runs away in panic; meets an old Moor who conducts her home; and learns later that the "little sheik" has been sent to prison for offering himself as a guide when he was not approved for that function by the municipality. As McKay says: ". . . in that country a native may catch prison as easy as a fly-paper a fly" (274).

The girl is a perfect example of McKay's vision of the pervasiveness of Western imperialism; she undoubtedly thinks of herself as an enlightened lover of the not "repulsive" "barbaric flower," and she could maintain correctly that she meant no one any harm. But her thoughtlessness does cause harm; and her very presence in that place and her attitude toward it are proof of the imperialistic power of the West. Her sexual fantasies are the result of a culturally induced view of the nonwhite as the personification of delightfully frightening eroticism. Little "independent U.S.A. girls" who have read too much cheap fiction follow in the wake of the invasion of American money and military power and cause their own kind of trouble. The story incidentally has special interest as one of McKay's few characterizations of an American white girl. However, it is finally not a successful piece of fiction; for both central characterizations are too stereotypical, the arrest of the "little sheik" is not well integrated into the plot, and McKay is is too discursive.

No one would probably maintain that McKay was a master of the short-story form, for several of the stories seem to have been written too hurriedly. Other stories, such as "Mattie and Her Sweetman," "Near-White," "Highball," "Crazy Mary," and "The Strange Burial of Sue," demonstrate, however, that McKay had real ability as a writer of short fiction. Moreover, *Gingertown* is interesting because McKay utilizes themes and attitudes found in his three novels. The style of the six Harlem stories is often similar to *Home to Harlem*; and the idea that varying shades of skin color have different spiritual and psychological effects upon Negroes is more fully realized in these six stories than in *Home to Harlem*, in which this concept is a subtheme. As strongly as *Banana Bottom*, the four Jamaican stories attack the Christian church as one of Western imperialism's main weapons against "black passion." Thus, while certainly not always McKay at his best, *Gingertown* is an important part of the body of his work.

CHAPTER 5

The Nonfiction: Harlem and the World

McKay's autobiography, *A Long Way From Home* (1937), and his sociological study, *Harlem: Negro Metropolis* (1940), are initially disappointing books. There is, however, much more value to the autobiography than to the study of Harlem. The key to both the disappointment and the merit of *A Long Way From Home* lies in the fact that it is not the usual kind of autobiography. If one approaches it expecting an intimate portrayal of Claude McKay, he will be disappointed; if he seeks in it an account of McKay's struggle to reconcile his views of art with his concepts of self, blackness, and the proletariat, he will find it valuable. *Harlem: Negro Metropolis* is more difficult to accept on any basis; for, while it contains some valuable insights into the major forces operative within the American and the world black communities, its last half is so full of passages of intensely vitriolic anger and despair aimed at the black intellectual establishment and at the Communist party that the entire book seems tinged with paranoia. This is not to say that there was no validity to McKay's bitterness toward black intellectuals and the Communist Party: it is simply to recognize that McKay's desperate need to attack these targets again and again overshadows the ostensible subject of the discussion. The book's supposed purpose of giving an objective account of the social and historical development of the New York black community is sidetracked; and the tone of the last half of the book is so overtly and desperately hostile that any artistic merit or sociological objectivity is destroyed.

In contrast to *Harlem*, *A Long Way From Home* ends on a hopeful, pacific note with one of McKay's most aesthetically satisfying discussions of black pride. In fact, the entire autobiography is written with such extreme restraint and control that the restraint becomes the book's main problem. One cannot argue that a complete shift occurred between 1937 and 1940 in McKay's emotional response to what he saw in black life because the defeatist tone of *Harlem: Negro Metropolis* is foreshadowed in the essay "Harlem Runs Wild" that was pulished in *The Nation* in 1935. Nevertheless, McKay's letters to Eastman do not reflect until around 1938 and 1939 the vitriolic, all-consuming anti-communism found in *Harlem* in 1940. Whatever the reasons, *A Long Way From Home* (1937), and especially its ending, represent McKay's last satisfying published prose statement of the assured black pride exhibited by Bita Plant.

Still, there is a level on which the autobiography is a disappointment. Rebecca Chalmers Barton makes two seemingly contradictory observations about *A Long Way From Home*: "The theme song of his [McKay's] life is his independence,"[1] and "Often his autobiography becomes a series of impressions and digressions about people, cities, women, art, politics and race."[2] While the discussions about art and race are not digressions, Barton is, in a sense, correct in both observations. One apparent theme of *A Long Way From Home* is McKay's refusal to be dominated by anyone. Ironically, however, one feels upon finishing the book that he has portrayed Frank Harris, Max Eastman, Charlie Chaplin, Edna St. Vincent Millay, Isadora Duncan, and numerous other famous and nonfamous personalities more clearly than he has Claude McKay. It would seem impossible for a man who is writing his autobiography to proclaim repeatedly his sense of independence and still fail to provide a complete and satisfactory view of himself as a personality. Nevertheless, that is precisely what happens in *A Long Way From Home*.

The irony of McKay's failure to depict himself adequately in his autobiography is compounded by the fact that, as previously discussed, his fiction often tends to become too overtly autobiographical. Frequently, he does not maintain an adequate distance between himself and his materials in his fiction, but he keeps too distant in his autobiography. This distance is especially disappointing if one approaches *A Long Way From Home* expecting an autobiography comparable to Richard Wright's *Black Boy*. In *Black Boy*, the nightmarish childhood, the romantic fantasies mingled with the sharply realistic sense of human and personal suffering, and the sheer impossibility of the odds overcome in Wright's triumph over his environment are all described with a detail often painful in its intimacy. While other characters (Wright's father, his mother, and various relatives) do emerge memorably, the focus of Wright's autobiography is always upon Wright. One feels certain that McKay felt as intensely and responded as deeply as Wright to the unique drama of his life; but, with the exception of a few major events, one does not get a sense of this intense personal response in *A Long Way From Home.*

McKay's reluctance to deal with the complexities of his own personal life does not prevent him from being convincing in his assertions of independence, but he does not assert his total independence from any and all larger groups. Barton makes another observation about the book that, when modified, is correct: she observes that McKay is obviously implying that what is important about himself is the fact that he is an artist; therefore, his artistic ideas and concerns transcend any details relevant only to his personal life.[3] This interpretation needs a significant qualification; what McKay really emphasizes is that he is a black artist, and his allegiance to his race does not contradict the theme of independence. Early in *A Long Way From Home,* McKay states that no artist can have a true sense of self unless that self is rooted in a nation or in a race. Thus, the Jamaican's sense of the uniqueness of Claude McKay and his feeling of belonging to the black race are inextricably linked. He does repeatedly, and convincingly, stress his independence from individuals and groups which attempt to control his individuality. These individuals and groups are predominantly white, either in actuality or in point of view. That Claude McKay could be the unique individualist and a black artist, just as Byron could be Byron and a distinctly English poet, is the book's final message. So Barton is wrong when she writes that McKay's "final loyalty is only to himself. . . ."[4] His final loyalty in the autobiography is to himself and to his blackness.

For all these reasons, the way to read *A Long Way From Home* is not as an autobiography but as literary theory accompanied by a view of the significant people, places, and events of a period. While McKay is persuasive in his assertion of his pride in self and in blackness, that self remains largely hidden behind a peculiar kind of restraint. Once again, it is the people McKay knew, including some potential destroyers of his individuality, who come the most alive in this book. In fact, *A Long Way From Home* opens with an almost complete concentration upon one of those people — a concentration that totally subordinates the first years of McKay's life and delays for over twenty-five pages the key statement of the interrelationship between the Jamaican's individuality and his blackness.

I A Long Way From Home

An indication that *A Long Way From Home* is not going to be the usual kind of autobiography comes immediately — McKay opens the book with a description of the thrilling impatience he underwent after receiving a letter in 1918 from Frank Harris requesting a meeting with McKay. McKay's job then was waiting tables for a railroad, and a run to Philadephia delayed the meeting by three days. In the course of describing the Philadelphia run, he summarizes in five sentences the years in Jamaica and in Kansas. There follows a very brief account of his five years as ". . . . a vagabond with a purpose,"[5] during which he survived by manual labor but always kept alive the desire to write. Moreover, his artistic goals had become specifically linked with America: "I desired to achieve something new, something in the spirit and accent of America. Against its mighty throbbing force, its grand energy and power and bigness, its bitterness burning in my black body, I would raise my voice to make a canticle of my reaction" (4). This attitude toward his adopted country is the same that appears so often in his fiction and poetry — admiration and respect for the limitless power of America, but hatred of its bigotry and prejudice. Throughout this account of his "vagabond" period and the growth of his specifically American literary ambitions, McKay periodically draws the reader's attention back to the fact that he carried a letter from Frank Harris in his pocket during that Philadelphia run.

The meeting with Harris was additionally delayed when, returned to New York, McKay learned that he had to join another crew immediately and was in Pittsburgh the next afternoon. The urge to meet Harris became so great that he could not sit still and went out on the streets of Pittsburgh, where he was mistakenly arrested as a draft dodger. Again McKay's major reaction to this experience, even to a night in a foul cell in the Pittsburgh jail, was frustration that it was keeping him from Harris. It is not difficult to understand the excitement that an ambitious young poet would feel when given the opportunity to meet an editor who did indeed have the power to make his career. But the effect of opening his autobiography with an account of his excitement about and his frustration in meeting Harris and with his subordination of the brief account of his early life to that event results in the feeling that Harris virtually created McKay. One feels that the Jamaican years and the "vagabond" years in America were important only as a preparation for the meeting with "a great editor." For instance, McKay tells us nothing of his marriage on July 30, 1914, in New York to his Jamaican childhood sweetheart, Eulalie Imelda Edwards; of their separation six months later, or of the birth of his daughter Ruth Hope whom he never saw.[6]

In addition, the significance of Jamaica is lessened by the intensely American nature of his creative ambition; and this attitude contains more than one irony. When McKay wrote his best novel, it was a Jamaican novel; and it was not long before Frank Harris, like everyone else, discovered that he could not control McKay. *Banana Bottom* and "Boyhood in Jamaica" are eloquent proof that growing up in Jamaica had a strong influence upon McKay; and Frank Harris was soon replaced by Max Eastman and *The Liberator* as a direct influence upon McKay. The complexity of McKay's life is perhaps illustrated in these facts: Harris and Eastman were only two of the many white men to "discover" and promote Claude McKay; Walter Jekyll had done it first, and later the entire Soviet Union attempted to make McKay theirs. Moreover, the theory of a black art with its roots in the masses contained in the three novels demonstrates that the "vagabond" years represented a vitally important period in McKay's life. By the second novel, McKay's subject matter has left America; and the focus is on an art that incorporates a *universal* black consciousness. And there is the poetry, part of which looks back romantically to Jamaica and part of which looks ahead prophetically to a universal blackness.

But the opening of *A Long Way From Home* ignores all these complexities, and one feels most the power and the presence of Frank Harris and of America. It is not too long before Harris and America are replaced by other individuals and places, though never Jamaica; but one of the two predominant motifs of the book is set. Already the autobiography's focus is on whom McKay is with and where he is; the intervals during which that focus shifts to McKay are far too rare. Moreover, most of those intervals are concerned, at least indirectly, with McKay's theory about the interrelationship between his art, his self, and his blackness, rather than with McKay, the person.

It is not surprising, therefore, that McKay initially viewed Harris as being almost equivalent with America in terms of sheer energy and power: "Frank Harris appeared to me then as the embodiment of my idea of a romantic luminary of the writing world. He stirred me sometimes like Byron and Heine, Victor Hugo and Rimbaud" (9). Their meeting, when it finally takes place, lasts all night and consists primarily in Harris' probing into McKay's past and in his lecturing him about his future. Whether McKay intends it or not, the main impression one takes away from this scene concerns the enormous ego of Harris — and, whether meant or not, of Harris as a parallel to America. But Harris does give the young poet some good advice: " 'You must write prose,' Frank said. I demurred. 'Yes, you must and you will,' he went on" (20). Then Harris added: " 'You are an African. You must accomplish things for yourself, for your race, for mankind, for literature . . .' " (21). How well McKay was to heed both these bits of advice — that he should write prose, and that he should be always conscious of his self and of his blackness — neither man could have anticipated at the time.

Harris also coaxes a confession from McKay about his reason for coming to America: "I admitted that back in my mind there had really been the dominant desire to find a bigger audience. Jamaica was too small for high achievements. There, one was isolated, cut off from the great currents of life" (20). That McKay wrote this passage after creating Bita Plant and that he never made any modification of this statement in the autobiography is intriguing and perplexing. One certainly understands a young writer's wanting "a bigger audience" and his living in New York, London, or Paris to find it. Young writers, black and white, have always done that. But no character McKay created is as much in tune with "the great currents of life" as Bita Plant, and none achieves more. On the other hand, one must admit that McKay could never have produced his first two novels or his best poetry had he not experienced the vitality of America and Europe.

At any rate, though McKay hardly needs to do so, he proclaims this evening with Harris as one of the great experiences of his life (22). Ironically, it is only a matter of weeks before the editor loses stature with the young poet; during a later meeting between the two in Harris' office, Harris suddenly says to McKay: " 'I am wondering whether your sensitivity is hereditary or acquired.' " McKay replies that it is probably "just human." The editor then explains why he asked the question: " 'What I mean is, the stock from which you stem — your people — are not sensitive. . . They have plenty of the instinct of the senses, much of which we have lost. But the attitude toward life is different; they are not sensitive about human life as we are. Life is cheap in Africa. . . .' " McKay says nothing after this speech, but Harris then explains that the greater "sensitivity" of Europeans to Africans is due to Jesus (23 - 24).

The ironic overtones of this scene are numerous and intriguing. First, of course, there is the strong element of Van Vechtenism in the comment about blacks' having retained more of their "instinct of the senses." But, second and more importantly, there is the hardly veiled implication that McKay is a kind of freak — Harris is asking how he can be both black and a sensitive artist. The Jamaican ran into this

kind of condescension all his life from his white promoters. But the
third and most inexplicable irony of all is McKay's reaction to Harris'
outburst. McKay, who was to state within the next twenty pages a
theory of the inseparability of his art and his blackness and who was
to write the very next year the most militantly black poem of the
Harlem Renaissance, answers that he regards European Christianity
as a hypocritical guise for imperialistic exploitation (24). One expects
a stronger reaction from McKay.

At least, one wants him not only to ask Harris how the editor
reconciles his theory of European "sensitivity" and concern for
human life with World War I but also to object to the implication
that a black artist is, by definition, almost an impossibility.
Amazingly, in fact, in recalling the incident McKay still seems to be
most upset because "in his role as a Jesus preacher the stature of
Frank Harris diminished perceptibly before my mind; the halo
around him that night when he talked as a rationalist and rebel
became less glamorous" (25). McKay makes it evident that Harris'
Christianity offends his philosophy of free thought infinitely more
than the editor's condescension affects his black pride.

McKay's reaction becomes even more perplexing when one considers that McKay is writing about this 1918 incident in the late
1930s; for there is little indication that the passage of the most artistically productive and creative years in McKay's life has modified
his inital reaction to Harris' tirade. McKay has in the interim created
characters and episodes that criticize Christianity, but he condemns
Harris on no other ground than the editor's advocacy of a
hypocritical, oppressive religion. An additional irony is, of course,
McKay's own conversion to Catholicism in the 1940s. This scene
with Harris illustrates the inconsistencies and complexities which the
student of McKay and particularly of A Long Way From Home encounters.

After Harris' speech about nonwhite insensitivity and McKay's
passive reaction to it, one is especially relieved to find almost immediately McKay's statement of the central thesis of A Long Way
From Home, as well as of virtually all his art. The statement is
prompted by another great man, the black critic and scholar William
Stanley Braithwaite. Braithwaite, in a letter, advises McKay to "send
to the magazines only such poems as did not betray [his] racial identity" (27). This advice results in the most significant passage in the
autobiography and in one of the most meaningful in all of McKay's
writing: "I felt more confidence in my own way because, of all the

poets I admire, major and minor, Byron, Shelley, Keats, Blake, Burns, Whitman, Heine, Baudelaire, Verlaine, and Rimbaud and the rest — it seemed to me that when I read them — in their poetry I could feel their race, their class, their roots in the soil, growing into plants, spreading and forming the backgrounds against which they were silhouetted. I could not feel the reality of them without that. So likewise I could not realize myself writing without conviction" (28).

This statement is a key to much that seems contradictory and confusing about McKay: he is saying that his art is to be a projection of his self as all great art represents the individuality of its creator, but that it is impossible to express that sense of self meaningfully without simultaneously depicting one's race, or country, or nationality. Every great artist has belonged to a nation, or larger group of some kind — Whitman to America, Keats to England, and Burns to Scotland. For McKay, no country was finally adequate to serve as the recipient of his group loyalty. He tried hard for much of his life to make America that country, he was drawn to England, he was impressed deeply by Russia, he was intrigued by North Africa, and he wrote his best book about Jamaica. But, in *A Long Way From Home*, universal black consciousness was his "final home," which was precisely why he was always "a long way from home" — he was seeking an as yet undiscovered country. It is significant that this passage overrules Ray's comment in *Banjo* that, if necessary, he will sacrifice his race to fulfill his art — black art, McKay says here, must result from an expression of the self as belonging to the race. This passage explains why McKay, in the remainder of *A Long Way From Home*, discusses his art sometimes in terms of his sense of self and sometimes in relation to blackness. Individuality and blackness are not contradictory; they are, in fact, complementary. As discussed in Chapter 2, this passage is also revealing in that all the poets mentioned as inspirations are white; the tension in McKay's own poetry between black content and traditional white form was inevitable.

Thus, a key to the related organizational and thematic principles of *A Long Way From Home* emerges; the book depicts all the people and ideologies that attempted to draw McKay away from his finally realized identity as a black artist. Harris and America are introduced, therefore, as initial recipients of McKay's loyalty and are then virtually dismissed. A seemingly curious aspect of the autobiography — that there is virtually no treatment in it of McKay's relationship with the black masses — is then explicable; for the story in *A Long Way From Home* is really about McKay's rejection of all that stood between him and his identification with the black common man.

After the Harris and Braithwaite episodes, the remainder of Part I centers upon McKay's alliance with Max Eastman and the *Liberator*, his friendship with a white criminal named Michael, and the increasing need for the young poet to leave America for a sojourn in England. Growing racial tension had much to do with McKay's desire to go to England; but, as Wayne Cooper and Robert C. Reinders indicate in their article, "A Black Briton Comes 'Home': Claude McKay in England, 1920," England had considerable attraction in itself for the young black poet. It represented three temptations away from black identity for McKay, two of which were to end immediately in bitter disillusionment. First, there was the possibility of contact with famous British "progressives," epitomized by McKay's long time idol, George Bernard Shaw; second, there was the appeal of the cultural capital for a "colonial"; and, third, there was socialist politics.[7]

The first two of these attractions — Shaw and the "colonial's" cultural center — immediately proved illusionary. McKay met Shaw, but the meeting was hardly one which could have encouraged the young Jamaican to have much faith in the English cultural tradition. During their conversation, Shaw suddenly asked McKay: " 'Why didn't you choose pugilism instead of poetry for a profession? . . . You might have developed into a successful boxer with training. Poets remain poor, unless they have an empire to glorify and popularize like Kipling.' I said that poetry had picked me as a medium instead of my picking poetry as a profession" (61). Shaw launched into a long discourse about cathedrals; and Cooper and Reinders write about the Shaw passage that, "At the risk of reading between the lines, it appears as if Shaw was bored with McKay and that McKay expected a great deal more from Shaw."[8] In *A Long Way From Home*, McKay expresses great admiration for Shaw's lecture on cathedrals and speaks admiringly of the British playwright in a personal letter to Max Eastman in May, 1925.[9] But this meeting with the author of *Saint Joan* represented virtually the whole of McKay's contact with the giants of British culture during his stay in London; and he could hardly have helped being disappointed.

In one of the poems in *Songs of Jamaica*, "Old England," McKay expresses a desire to visit his true cultural "homeland," England. With the names of Shakespeare, Milton, Wordsworth all ringing in his mind since his poetic apprenticeship in Jamaica, McKay obviously went to England expecting to find a nation of tolerance and culture. What he found was racism as blatant as that in the United States; indeed, Cooper and Reinders refer to McKay's experience as ". . . a case study of the disillusioned colonial."[10] Ironically, the sharpest attacks on English racism in *A Long Way From Home* are related to boxing: McKay met a promising black boxer who had a white wife, and he observed the brutal humiliation to which they were exposed. For proof that McKay never recovered from the shock of English racism, one need only cite his exchange of letters with Max Eastman near the end of his life when he refused to retract his charge that England and America were more guilty of vicious international racism than the Soviet Union, and these letters were written long after McKay's disillusionment with Russia and the Communist party. In fact, McKay always remained infinitely more hostile toward England than toward the United States. He returned to America and a part of him always responded to it; in his letters to Eastman, he always speaks of England and the British Empire in a purely vitriolic tone. Only in the posthumously published "Boyhood in Jamaica," does one find McKay writing about England with some of his former admiration.

However, it was in England that McKay's association with leftist politics really began; and that was to be the strongest of the ideologies which tempted him from his "home" in black consciousness until his conversion to Roman Catholicism at the end of his life. In fact, much of McKay's life can be regarded as a desperate, and finally unsuccessful, attempt to make his loyalties to blackness and to the proletariat inseparable. As mentioned in Chapter 1, at London's International Club, he discovered Marx and then, by writing a fiery answer to a series of *Daily Herald* black-scare editorials, he became involved with Sylvia Pankhurst, the *Workers' Dreadnought*, and the British Socialist movement. Cooper and Reinders provide an excellent discussion of McKay's *Dreadnought* contributions: they were invariably about racial questions and displayed an inflexible independence of opinion.[11]

The *Dreadnought* experience was meaningful to McKay. In a letter to Eastman written from Petrograd on May 18, 1923, McKay challenged a remark by Eastman that the Jamaican was never oriented toward politics: "If you had seen me standing on street corners and selling red literature in London 1920 - 21, you would not make such a funny remark."[12] Even though some years later McKay told Eastman that he had never been political, leftist politics were for a while a very serious matter to McKay. In fact, as Cooper and Reinders indicate, "McKay deserves a footnote in British history as the first Negro Socialist to write for a British periodical."[13] From England McKay returned to America minus any faith in British culture, but with a new commitment to International Socialism. Parts III and IV of *A Long Way From Home* represent his attempt to wed that commitment with his black identity, first with Eastman and the *Liberator* in New York, and then during "the magic pilgrimage" to Russia.

The opening of Part III of the autobiography concerns the poet's return to New York, and it contains one of the few really intimate glimpses of McKay: "It was good to be lost in the shadows of Harlem again. It was an adventure to loiter down Fifth and Lenox avenues and promenade along Seventh Avenue. Spareribs and corn pone, fried chicken and corn fritters and sweet potatoes were like honey to my palate"(96). After McKay's tribute to one of his lovers — the enchanting West Indian girl Sanina—he shifts to the *Liberator* experience and to Eastman, Floyd Dell, and Mike Gold who were his associates on the journal. Nonetheless, the independence which McKay always exhibited while associated with the *Liberator* is reflected in certain passages such as the account of his insistence upon printing the poetry of e.e. cummings despite the objections of assistant editor, Robert Minor; and his statement to Minor that he always kept his "social sentiments" and his "esthetic emotions" separate (102 - 3). This last assertion is not really true, for McKay has already said that his blackness and his art are inextricably bound together; but his statement to Minor does foreshadow his inevitable clash with proletarian theories of art.

The climax to the *Liberator* episode comes with McKay's account of his experience in being sent to the balcony of a theater when he went (with orchestra tickets) to review *He Who Gets Slapped* for the *Liberator*, and his resulting fiery editorial about public discrimination: "Shock them out of their complacency, Blackface; make them uncomfortable; make them unhappy! Give them no peace, no rest. How can they bear your presence, Blackface, great, unappeasable ghost of Western civilization!" (145). So painful was this experience that McKay could stand America no longer, and he decided to visit the Soviet Union.

In certain ways, Part IV of the autobiography, which recounts the Russian experience, is the climax of *A Long Way From Home*.

Russia brought McKay face to face with the temptations of the Communist party and loyalty to the universal proletariat. In describing McKay's year in Moscow (1922 - 1923), Stephen H. Bronz writes that "Perhaps most of all he was a fascinated and lionized tourist. . . . It is no wonder that Communists often found McKay deficient as a proletarian poet. McKay was enchanted by the exotic remnants of Moscow's past, and even his praise of Lenin seems to be more admiration for a great historical figure than for a great Communist leader."[14] Some truth exists in this assessment, but it is an oversimplification. McKay did believe in Marxism during the period of the Russian pilgrimage and for a period thereafter; in a letter to Eastman dated May, 1925, he states that, while he does not care for openly propagandistic writing, he is ". . . a revolutionist of the communist persuasion because it happens at this period to be the most progressive and and [sic] reasonable *from the proletarian viewpoint* which I accept."[15]

The same letter, however, already reveals disillusionment with Russia as an example of proletarian reform; for McKay praises Eastman for working to remove the proletarian movement from Moscow's control.[16] One should also remember Ray's remarks in *Home to Harlem* about the supreme historical importance of the Russian Revolution. McKay, converted by reading Marx in London, obviously went to Russia to see the fulfillment of a political dream he then shared. However, despite much that was pleasant about the "pilgrimage," he encountered two sources of disillusionment: the oppression of the former Czarists by the Soviet government, and the Moscow insistence that writers should write acceptable party propaganda. The time-gap between the events described in the Russian section and the time of the writing of *A Long Way From Home* raises interesting questions. As mentioned, McKay's letters to Eastman between approximately 1925 and 1937 reveal a growing animosity toward the Moscow government and Marxist literary critics, but they do not reflect the consuming suspicion and hatred toward everything he imagined to be related to Communism that begins to dominate the correspondence around 1938. In the years prior to the publication of *A Long Way From Home,* he was not yet proclaiming to Eastman that he had never been a Communist or that Communism was "a primitive ideal."

Thus, in the autobiography, McKay can still recall the Russian visit with some real pleasure; Bronz correctly states that McKay was "lionized" by party officials and by the Russian masses alike. As mentioned in Chapter 1, he curiously does not mention his speech to the Third Communist International. Though McKay's dislike of the Soviet bureaucracy and the Marxist literary critics had grown even more intense since 1922 -1923, the treatment accorded him by everyone from Trotsky to the man on the Moscow streets still evoked pleasant memories. The tone in which he recounts these memories is why Bronz refers to him as having been a "tourist" in Russia. Yet, what the Russian section of the autobiography really reveals is that McKay went to the Soviet Union as a believer in Marxism *and* that he was inevitably going to become disillusioned with the proletarian movement.

In recounting the welcome given him by the Russian masses, he writes, "My response was as sincere as the mass feeling was spontaneous. That miraculous experience was so extraordinary that I have never been able to understand it" (167). Moreover, he remembers his reception by the Bolshevist officialdom with an almost equal pleasure. Trotsky is described as ". . . human and universal in his outlook" (182). And, in perhaps the strongest statement of McKay's positive response to the Russian experience, he even admits the necessity for that Soviet bureaucracy which he was later to despise so intensely. The Russian visit obviously meant a great deal to McKay.

But another aspect of McKay's visit is just as clear. Throughout his experience in Russia, he resisted pressure from Soviet officials to become a Party member and, except for the one speech, to become a symbol of communist influence within the American black community. In his autobiography, McKay always describes the refusal as being based on his assertion that he is a "poet," not a political figure. Moreover, the Jamaican refused consistently to reassure the Russian bureaucrats that an American proletarian revolution was imminently forthcoming or that conditions for the American worker were as bad as the Soviet officialdom wanted to believe. He was, in fact, greatly amused at the manner in which Jack London's novel *The Iron Heel* was accepted by Russians as a realistic picture of American society. Finally, his sympathy for the people once loyal to the Czar and now oppressed by the Communists increased the longer he remained in the Soviet Union.

Seemingly, McKay went to Russia to view a great social experiment with which he was sympathetic; but he realized that the experiment was, in reality, not an answer to his own problems. He soon felt it necessary to leave: "The thought of leaving seemed to be the most logical. I knew myself enough to know that I was not of the stuff of a practical pioneer, who could become a link in that mighty chain of the upbuilding of the great Russian revolution" (203). The *great* Russian revolution, yes — but, finally, not *his* revolution. The real reason for both McKay's inability to commit himself to the Party in 1922 - 1923 and for his ultimate rejection of the proletarian movement is hinted at in a postscript to the Soviet pilgrimage entitled "Regarding Radical Criticism." In it, McKay answers a *New Masses* criticism of his writing; the Marxist critic had, in effect, denounced McKay's novels and poems as being irresponsibly lacking in " 'working-class content.' "

McKay focuses his defense around *Home to Harlem* and argues that he created Jake as a realistic example of black working-class life and defies "the Communists" to create a more realistic example. At one point during his account of the Russian period, McKay describes his lecture to an American mulatto delegate to the International Congress in which he had asserted that the only answer for the American Negro lay in a separate and highly organized black political power group (177 - 78). Such a sentiment hardly constitutes an expression of faith in the universal proletariat. This speech to the mulatto delegate and the postscript defense of his writing indicate that the real source of McKay's discontent was the *beginning* of his realization in 1922 - 1923, that the concept of a universal proletariat was not the solution to the black man's struggle. Thus, when McKay continually insisted to the Soviet officials that he was a "poet" and not a politician, he was really saying that he was not, and never could be, their poet. Partially he was asserting his independence as Claude McKay; but he was also expressing, however obliquely, a higher loyalty to blackness.

That McKay continued for a few years to cling to the illusion that Marxism was the answer for the black man and that, even when that illusion was shattered, he still wrote about the trip to Russia with a degree of affectionate nostalgia should not be too surprising. For, until the last few years of his life and until his conversion to Catholicism, the concept of proletarian revolution was the strongest of all his temptations to desert his belief in pure black identity. After all, his Marxist sympathies had involved him in writing for the *Workers' Dreadnought* in England and the *Liberator* in America. Shortly after the publication of *A Long Way From Home*, he was to come to the conclusion that the universal proletariat concept was not only irrelevant to the black struggle, but actually antithetical to it;

and, when he reached that degree of disillusionment, he became a vehement anti-Communist. But Marx represented a dream that held a great deal of appeal for McKay during some vital years. Thus, the years 1922 and 1923 were as crucial as any period in McKay's life: the visit to Russia represented the climax of his attempt to follow the Marxist ideal, and the beginning of his disillusionment in that same ideal. Not surprisingly like a great many other people, McKay attempted for a while to believe in abstract Communism after his loss of faith in the Soviet government.

Like Harris and America, Shaw and England, Eastman and the *Liberator,* Russia and Lenin and Trotsky failed to be the "home" McKay was seeking. Part V of *A Long Way From Home,* entitled "The Cynical Continent," describes the period from 1923 to 1930 in which McKay drifted about Europe and was an expatriate whose experience is somewhat comparable to that of famous white American writers such as Hemingway and Stein. Indeed, part of the focus of Part V is on the white American expatriates and McKay's relationship to them. Perhaps even more than in any other section of the book, other people and places overshadow McKay in Part V; one rarely gets a view of McKay, the expatriate, except in a very abstract way. However, McKay does make it clear that he never fully identified with the white expatriates largely because of racial difference. In addition, he simply did not share the causes so dear to most of the white "exiles": he had not yet totally rejected America as they had ("For I was in love with the large rough unclassical rhythms of American life" [244]); he was not really concerned about American lack of appreciation for the artist or about the stifling nature of American puritanism ("The puritan atmosphere of America was irritating, but it was not suffocating" [244]); and he was not rebelling against America in the name of sexual freedom ("And lastly, sex was never much of a problem to me. I played at sex as a child in a healthy harmless way" [244 - 45]). McKay's "problem" was simply "color-consciousness"; and, while the white expatriates were sympathetic, they could not understand the reality of the black experience.

Probably a contributing factor to McKay's inability to respond to the white expatriates is hinted at in one of the few personal insights into McKay's European life. While most of the white Americans were financially comfortable, or at least secure, McKay was reduced to posing nude in Paris art studios to survive. The poorly heated studios gave him pneumonia, which contributed to the poor health which plagued him the rest of his life.

After the account of his inability to be a real poet of the expatriate experience, McKay discusses the literary lions of the 1920s. He admired Joyce tremendously: "If I were to label James Joyce I would say that he was (in the classic sense of the word) a great Decadent" (247). However, Lawrence was his favorite modern writer. He felt no admiration for Gertrude Stein either as the "madame" of the expatriate movement or as a writer; he refused several invitations to her house and regarded "Melanctha" as an obviously superficial story of black life. As already discussed, he not only admired Hemingway, but to some degree identified with him.

After these descriptions, McKay spends most of the remainder of Part V in relating anecdotes about famous personalities of the 1920s. Meetings with Harold Sterns, Edna St. Vincent Millay (". . . I saw her as a Shakespearean woman deftly adapted to the modern machine age. When I searched for an Anglo-Saxon word to fix her in my mind I could think of 'elfin' only" [258 - 59]), Sinclair Lewis, and others are recounted. Frank Harris reappears briefly along with the Max Eastmans. Finally, the scene shifts to Marseilles and to some *Banjo*-like descriptions of the waterfront. The celebrity game intrudes even here, however; Isadora Duncan appears with a lover; and the two, along with McKay, explore the vice center of the city.

While the emphasis upon famous acquaintances overshadows this section of the autobiography, the most meaningful aspect of Part V in terms of the book as a whole is McKay's account of his attraction to the expatriate movement and his final inability to commit himself to it. The book's central motif of describing the temptations away from black consciousness and the inevitable rejection of them is kept intact.

Book VI is largely centered in North Africa, an area to which McKay responded intensely, but which was still not "home." For a time Morocco did seem to be the place McKay had always been seeking; there among the natives he was free for the first time in his life from the oppression of racism. But he could not isolate himself among the natives; the power of the French and the English was present in North Africa. McKay's radical past, and the Russian experience, were well known; and he was always regarded suspiciously by British and French colonial officials. As his letters to Eastman indicate, this experience with European imperialism in Africa contributed much to McKay's lifelong hatred of European imperialism. There was more, however, behind McKay's failure to make North Africa a home than appears in the autobiography. He was broke, sick, and lonely; he felt removed from the cultural centers where he hoped to make a literary comeback. *Banana Bottom* flopped during his stay in Morocco, and he felt the need more intensely than ever to return to a place where he might have a chance to prove himself again as a writer. But, in the autobiography, the sense of imperialistic persecution gets the emphasis.

A tone strikingly different from the often desperate letters written to Eastman from Morocco is apparent in Book VI of *A Long Way From Home*. Looking back on the North African experience from an American vantage point, McKay remembers it as being perhaps better than it was in actuality: ". . . I experienced more of purely physical happiness than at any time in my life" (333); and his account of the North African years ends with a tribute to the "magical barbaric" Moroccans (338). Obviously, McKay did respond deeply to the North Africans; but the personal suffering and the loneliness he felt while in Morocco seemingly have been forgotten in *A Long Way From Home*.

It was inevitable that McKay would try to find a "home" in Africa — the exponent of art based upon black consciousness was simply looking back to the mother continent. But, even while he responded to the "magical barbaric" Moroccans, he was, by education and profession, dependent upon that white "civilization" of America which refused to treat him as an equal human being. Thus McKay, like Wright and Baldwin after him, found that Africa was not to be the answer to the tragic "duality" implicit in the Afro-American heritage. Even though Part VI of *A Long Way From Home* seems to imply that McKay could have been indefinitely happy in Morocco had the British and French authorities left him alone, this implication is almost certainly not true. The tone of Part VI is probably due to the understandable bitterness McKay felt toward America almost immediately upon his return. Life in the States was infinitely more cruel to him after his return in 1934 than it had been before his departure in 1922; thus, he might well have looked back upon North Africa with considerable nostalgia. Though he never left America again after 1934, he was never able to consider it "home."

At one point during his stay in Morocco, he was asked his nationality and replied, "I said I was born in the West Indies and lived in the United States and that I was an American, even though I was a British subject, but I preferred to think of myself as an internationalist." When asked to define "internationalist," he answered that ". . . an internationalist was a bad nationalist" (300). McKay was always a very "bad nationalist" simply because the "home" he found during the writing of his three novels and his autobiography was black consciousness and no one nation, not even Morocco, could encompass that. It is a supreme irony, but again one faced by more than one later Afro-American writer, that circumstances and education finally made it necessary for McKay to attempt to pursue that consciousness within a white civilization. The facts that he needed to eat and to talk to other writers and that he thought he could do those two things better in America than in Africa do not negate his commitment to blackness; they simply emphasize the problems inherent in McKay's and virtually every other Afro-American or West Indian intellectual's dilemma. For balance, one must also point out that McKay derived a great deal of pleasure from his friendship with such white intellectuals as the Eastmans.

Indeed, the two most intriguing single chapters in Part VI are not specifically related to the Moroccan experience: the first, "The New Negro in Paris," states McKay's lack of identification with the Harlem Renaissance leadership; the second, "On Belonging to a Minority Group," serves as an appropriate end to the autobiography because it emphasizes the commitment of his art to the black masses. In "The New Negro in Paris," McKay states the essential disagreement between himself and the Renaissance intelligentsia; and, were it not for McKay's obvious antipathy toward the DuBois-Locke position, it would be about as cogent a statement as possible of the differences, as McKay defends *Home to Harlem* against the charge of its being degrading to the race:

My idea of a renaissance was one of talented persons of an ethnic or national group working individually or collectively in a common purpose and creating things that would be typical of their group.
I was surprised when I discovered that many of the talented Negroes regarded their renaissance more as an uplift organization and a vehicle to accelerate the pace and progress of smart Negro society. . . .
Also, among the Negro artists there was much of that Uncle Tom attitude which works like Satan against the idea of a coherent and purposeful Negro group. Each one wanted to be the first Negro, the one Negro, and the only Negro *for the whites* instead of for their group (321 - 22).

The implication that the Renaissance leaders were intent on "selling out" to the whites to promote black society is patently unfair to men like DuBois and Locke, but the statement that McKay could never view an artistic movement as an "uplift organization" identifies the basic disagreement quite well.

"On Belonging to a Minority Group," McKay's most satisfying essay about black pride, begins by answering a charge by Nancy
Cunard that his novels rested on a concept of racial pride that
limited their enjoyment by a white reader: "It leaves me wondering
whether it would be altogether such a bad thing if by ringing itself in
closer together, a weak, disunited and suppressed group of people
could thereby develop group pride and strength and self-respect!"
(345). Then he attacks the issue of white aid to black progress:
"Well, whatever the white folks do and say, the Negro race will
finally have to face the need to save itself. The whites have done the
blacks some great wrongs, but also they have done some good. They
have brought to them the benefits of modern civilization. They can
still do a lot more, but one thing they cannot do: they cannot give
Negroes the gift of a soul — a group soul" (349). One remembers
McKay's long-standing commitment to black community solidarity
and Kent's argument that, while McKay never recommended the
rejection of all aspects of white civilization, he still found it to be
morally shallow and hypocritical. One essential message of his novels
is the necessity of a black "group soul"; indeed, to help bring that
soul into being was the overriding purpose behind their creation.
Next, the "uplift" issue is once more attacked: ". . . the Negro intelligentsia cannot hope to get very far if the Negro masses are
despised and neglected" (351).

Finally, McKay asserts the inevitability of black group-
consciousness and discusses his dream of being a prophet for such an
emerging racial consciousness. McKay "comes home" at the end of
his autobiography, and his "home" is black consciousness that rests
firmly in faith in the Negro masses. Moveover, his idea of his use of
his art in the search for black identity and power is a statement of the
basic purpose behind his novels and much of his poetry. The
autobiography completes, therefore, the period of McKay's greatest
achievement — in the years 1919 to 1937, he produced the work that
made him one of the most prophetic black writers of his time.
Reading *A Long Way From Home* in this light enables one to accept
it as a meaningful statement of artistic principle and to understand
its apparent failure as autobiography. If one is not allowed an intimate perception of McKay the man, he does find an account of the
essential beliefs of McKay the black artist. Moreover, he is shown all
the people, places, and ideologies that threated to draw McKay away
from black consciousness; the fact that these false gods often eclipse
McKay in the narration demonstrates their strength and thereby

makes their rejection all the more meaningful. In this light, even the opening scene with Frank Harris is at least somewhat acceptable; but a better title for the book would have been *The Gods that Failed*. In less than ten years, McKay painfully found another "home" in Catholicism, and he repudiated most of his fiction devoted to black consciousness. Neither in poetry nor in prose was he to regain real artistic power.

II Harlem: Negro Metropolis

In 1939, McKay lost his position with the Federal Writers' Project of the Works Progress Admimistration because of his status as an "alien:" he had not yet acquired American citizenship papers. He felt, however, that there was more involved; in a letter to Eastman, he blames the dismissal on "Communist" officials in the WPA.[17] He had already sent his publishers, Harper's, the manuscript of *Harlem: Negro Metropolis* at the time of this letter, and he expresses fear about the book's acceptance because "I can't get down the thought of the Communist sympathizers who are camouflaged everywhere!" Although the letter reflects McKay's state of mind during the period of the writing of *Harlem: Negro Metropolis*, his Federal Writers Project experience certainly did not produce overnight his deepseated belief that a "Stalinist" conspiracy had permeated all aspects of American society: the Eastman correspondence reveals as early as January, 1939, his fear of "Stalinists" in America.

In fact, McKay's 1935 essay in *The Nation*, "Harlem Runs Wild," had discussed the Communists' attempt to seduce the Harlem masses. This essay is focused around the attempt by Sufi Abdul Hamid to organize an effective black-labor coalition in New York and upon the destruction of Hamid by the Communists, the black intelligentsia, and the Jewish merchants. There is a striking difference, however, between McKay's essay and his 1939 letters to Eastman: in "Harlem Runs Wild," McKay is much more anxious to attack the Negro intellectuals and the Jewish businessmen than the Communists. In fact, he views the Communists in 1935 as a sinister, but rather ineffectual, force in Harlem. In the last chater of *Harlem: Negro Metropolis*, McKay also deals with the destruction of the Sufi Abdul Hamid movement; but, while the black intelligentsia is still treated harshly, the Communists are seen as a much more dangerous and powerful force.

In another way, the tone of "Harlem Runs Wild" clearly anticipates *Harlem: Negro Metropolis*. In the essay, occasioned by a race riot in Harlem, McKay regards the riot as ". . . the gesture of a bewildered, baffled, and disillusioned people"[18]; he is reluctant to give it any more significance than that; and he commends the police for keeping it under control.[19] One cannot help but contrast this response to a race riot to the proud defiance of "If We Must Die" in 1919 or, for that matter, to the ending of *A Long Way From Home* which appeared two years *later* and which insisted upon the inevitability of a powerful Negro group-consciousness. In one of the most revealing comments in the essay, McKay asserts that the factors behind the failure of Hamid's movement ". . . are as obscure and inscrutable as the composite mind of the Negro race itself."[20] It is as if McKay had given up even trying to comprehend his own race. *A Long Way From Home* is the exceptional product of McKay's post-1934 career — it is a statement of a black pride as undiluted as that contained in the novels. On the other hand, *Harlem: Negro Metropolis* has the defeatist tone of the 1935 essay and adds to it a vitriolic anti-Communism. This tone makes McKay's attacks upon the Negro intellectual leadership sound petty and mean.

The initial attraction that Marxism held for McKay and his subsequent bitter disillusionment with the party parallel the experiences of Richard Wright, Ralph Ellison, and others. There was more than a little validity to McKay's feeling that both the national and international party sought to use the black man. As already discussed, his animosity toward the black intellectual establishment began with the critical reception of *Home to Harlem*, if not before; and there are manifestations of this antipathy in virtually all of his prose. In fact, McKay's desperate preoccupation with these matters — the need to refer to them no matter how arbitrarily — not only mars the tone of *Harlem: Negro Metropolis* but also separates it from McKay's better work.

The first two chapters of the book, "Harlem Vista" and "The Negro Quarter Grows Up," are an interesting, if overly abstract, discussion of the history and significance of Negro Harlem. Three ideas dominate these introductory chapters: "Harlem *is* lacking in group solidarity and the high seriousness of other Aframerican communities";[21] nevertheless, because of its diversity and geographical location, "it is the Negro capital of the world" and ". . . the most interesting sample of black humanity marching along with white humanity" (16); and it possesses unique sociological value because, more than in any other minority community in the world, "individuals of achievement and wealth" are physically unable to escape the common man and establish "an oasis of respectability"(23).

The book's initial tone makes it obvious that McKay finds it difficult to believe, as the ending of *A Long Way From Home* suggests, that "group solidarity" will inevitably be attained in black America; moreover, he now views Harlem's lack of "high seriousness" as a much greater failing than he did in *Home to Harlem*. The last two ideas — that Harlem is more interesting and sociologically important than any other black community because it is a Negro settlement surrounded by a powerful white city and because of its leveling effect on the social aspirations of its own upper classes — underlie McKay's fiction and do not reflect the bitterness of the overall study. Indeed, the concept that Harlem inevitably influences and is influenced by white New York is developed as positively as anything in the book. The idea carries an implication of hope in regard to race relations that is surprising in view of the tone of *Harlem: Negro Metropolis*, as well as that of the letters McKay wrote to Eastman in the late 1930s. The discussion of the "talented tenth's" inability to escape physically from the black masses is distinguished by the same attitude of irreverent amusement that underlies *Home to Harlem*.

The third chapter is an account of the colorful career of Father Divine, and the first half of it is the most interesting part of *Harlem: Negro Metropolis*. McKay's predominant attitude toward his subject is a highly effective mixture of amusement at the Negro charlatan's nerve and guile and admiration of his ability to disturb the white and black establishments. Also, in discussing Divine's appeal, McKay takes the same stance toward religion that dominates the account of his conversion to Catholicism in the Eastman letters: people who can not understand the Father Divine phenomenon have not analyzed ". . . the non-intellectual conception of God," he asserts. Of course, this approach to spiritual matters is in keeping with the Jamaican's lifelong commitment to things emotional and intuitive.

But McKay's need to attack the Communist party wherever possible soon controls the narrative about Father Divine, for McKay shifts into an account of the Communists' unsuccessful attempt to manipulate the God of Harlem for their own ends. The tone becomes positively gleeful when McKay writes that, instead, Divine tricked the Party and used it to promote his own cause. McKay even compares the "platforms" of the "Stalinists" and of Father Divine as being based upon a comparable hypocrisy. The validity of McKay's analysis of Divine's relationship with the Party and of the two movements' similar appeal is really not important. What matters and what is destructive to the effectiveness of McKay's book is his compulsive need to transform his discussion about a unique and fascinating personality into an anti-Communist tirade and to make his charges of collusion between Divine and "the Stalinists" with no proof or convincing support. In the last half of the chapter, one learns much more about McKay's hostility to the Party than he does about the God of Harlem.

The religions and the supernatural cults of Harlem and its legitimate and illegitimate business endeavors are treated in the next four chapters. The appeal of the instinctual and the emotional which once occasioned McKay to call himself a pagan now underlies his sympathetic analysis of black Christianity: "Negroes, being human, love religion and also being animals, they wallow in animism. The religious heart of the Negro is his golden gift to America. . . . Some choniclers believe that Negro religion is the nearest thing extant to the primitive religion of Jesus" (73).

McKay moves without much difficulty from this point to an attack on the Negro intelligentsia: "[Black intellectuals] . . . fondly delude themselves that there is no difference between black folks' religion and white folks' religion — just as they can hypnotize themselves into thinking that there is no difference between white and black" (73). In truth, McKay asserts, Harlem religion is overwhelmingly dominated by the emotional appeal of a "magic" whose roots can be traced to the mother continent of Africa; and Harlem's numerous dealers in the occult are simply carrying on the tradition of obeahism and voodooism (73 - 75). In discussing both the legitimate black business ventures of Harlem and the "numbers" racket, McKay emphasizes the oppressive power of white capital; for Harlem is plagued by a "chronic sickness" that is the result of white ownership of most of its business establishments.

This analysis of Harlem's commercial plight, which constitutes an early plea for black economic power and independence, is perhaps the most far-sighted aspect of McKay's book. He supports his point of the necessity of black capital by asserting that "an analysis of the popular movements of Harlem [Garvey, Divine, the numbers racket] show that they all spring from the simple instinctive urge of the Negro masses to support some form of community enterprise" (90). While the tone of the remainder of the book indicates a loss of faith in the possibility of Harlem's ever attaining adequate economic power, McKay realizes the necessity of struggling for such power. Specifically in regard to "the business of numbers," the Jamaican writes that, when the white gang took over, "the éclat . . . went out of the game forever" (112). Such a statement reflects the old irreverent McKay who was the despair of the Renaissance proponents of "uplift."

When the Jamaican next turns to a discussion of Harlem's cabarets and other centers of amusement, one is inevitably reminded of *Home to Harlem* and expects a comparable tribute to "the joy stuff" of the black belt. But the writer is now the McKay of the late 1930s, not the creator of Jake and Felice; therefore, the chapter is in keeping with the preceding discussions of white capital in Harlem and focuses on white control of black entertainment and entertainers. Its tone and thesis call to mind such subsequent narratives about the suffering of black performers as that of John A. Williams' *Night Song.*

In the next chapter, entitled "Harlem Politician," McKay's tone of irrational bitterness really begins to dominate the book. After the Father Divine discussion, McKay's arguments are generally reasonable and often far-sighted until the "Harlem Politician" chapter. There are interesting passages concerning the history of the Tammany-Republican struggle for Negro votes and the political rivalry between native-born blacks and West Indians. In his analysis of the native-born/West-Indian conflict, McKay becomes preoccupied with shooting at an old target: "The educated American Negro is brought up in the tradition of special protection and patronage for the talented members of his group. He regards the West Indian as an outsider, who should not share in the special patronage."

However, like all immigrants, the West Indian has a special sensitivity about the subtle workings of the social system and advances politically beyond the native-born American black man. Inevitably, bitterness results: "It was natural that the exclusive tenth among the native-born would be a little resentful" (132). Undeniably, some personal rancor exists in McKay's account of the West Indian's being put in the role of outsider by "the exclusive tenth." While he had understandable reasons for resenting the Negro intelligentsia, his compulsion to turn a superficially related discussion into a diatribe against them weakens the plausibility of *Harlem: Negro Metropolis.* Throughout this chapter, the same compulsive need appears when McKay discusses a proposal to build an all-black hospital in Harlem which would be in the great tradition of Booker T. Washington; McKay asserts the project is being sidetracked by ". . . the obstreperous and extremely vocal and effective group of Negro intellectuals who style themselves the 'anti-Segregationists' " (124).

Somehow the discussion turns to the Schomburg black collection at the 135th Street branch library: "Ironically, this priceless affirmation of the culture of the Negro group has been disparaged by some of its intellectuals as a segregated institution" (140). One grants the thesis that certain aspects of black identity and integrity are too valuable to sacrifice in the name of a largely illusory concept of integration; still, the unsupported and vitriolic nature of these largely tangential passages offends. McKay is being no fairer to the DuBois position than DuBois was to him in the famous review of *Home to Harlem*.

McKay's last two chapters, which constitute approximately one half of the book, are concerned with the Garvey movement and the attempt by Sufi Abdul Hamid to organize the black workers of Harlem. McKay's attitude toward Garvey had changed since he dismissed the "Back to Africa" spokesman in *Banjo* as a "fool, big-mouf nigger." In *A Long Way From Home*, Garvey is regarded as a "charlatan," but one "who aroused the social consciousness of the Negro masses more than any leader ever did." In *Harlem: Negro Metropolis*, McKay is still not ready to accept Garvey, the man, completely; but he does focus upon the positive contribution that the West Indian leader's movement made to black pride. Nevertheless, the discussion of the "Back to Africa" movement is disappointing, essentially because it degenerates too often into a bitter attack upon the black intelligentsia whom McKay sees as contributing significantly to Garvey's downfall.[22] The primary motivation which McKay attributes to the Negro intellectuals for opposing Garvey is jealousy over the West Indian's ability to exact loyalty from the black masses.

The long final chapter concerning the attempts by Sufi Abdul Hamid and others to organize black labor in Harlem rests on two perceptive ideas. First, McKay argues that the old-guard black intelligentsia opposed all attempts to create viable black unions out of a fear of condoning segregation. Second, he treats the inevitable tension in the Communist party's attitude toward the black man; given the racist nature of much of the white proletariat, McKay argues that the party could not and did not really want to improve the Negro's economic condition. The white worker would view every job that the party might obtain for a black laborer as a blow to his own economic security. McKay had been aware of this inevitable conflict as far back as *Banjo*.

Anyone familiar with the assimilationist overtones of most black writing of the period from 1890 to 1920 sees the truth of McKay's first point. Too often, the Negro intellectual of the generation preceding McKay's had been willing to renounce real racial unity for the promise of increased integration. A book like Chesnutt's *The Marrow of Tradition* is a particularly striking example of this tendency, and one notices the same thing in much of DuBois's *early* writing. When McKay called for a greater emphasis on economic progress attained through black unity, he was being undeniably progressive; and equally farsighted is his insight into the reasons behind the Communist party's often cynical manipulations of the black man.

Had McKay utilized objective support in developing these points, he might have produced an incisive essay. But the poverty, literary obscurity, and personal illness of his life in America had produced a state of mind in the late 1930s that made such objectivity impossible. His tendency to see "Stalinists" everywhere is apparent in this last essay, and his denunciations of the black intelligentsia become so frequent and bitter that one begins to view them sympathetically because of reaction to McKay's shrill attack. As in the Father Divine essay, McKay becomes preoccupied with the concept of collusion; he accuses the black intellectuals of more or less consciously aiding the Party in its undermining of viable Negro unions. He refers to ". . . the Communists, Socialists and the defeatist horde of the Negro intelligentsia who had opposed the crude yet constructive efforts of the black masses to organize themselves" (228).

Toward the end of the chapter, he asserts that black intellectuals really do not want the racial situation improved: ". . . the intellectuals apparently find psychic satisfaction in a tangle of race problems and in resistance to the sane measures which may eventually untangle them" (255). To the degree that McKay's comment is meant to apply to a man like DuBois, it is obviously unfair. One has to go no farther back in McKay's career than *A Long Way From Home* to find him able to debate his opponents without indulging in the compulsion to label them as fools at best, and traitors to the race at the worst. Increasingly, name-calling, instead of objective argumentation, dominates this last chapter.

Obviously, McKay's virtually unrelieved suffering after his return to the United States had brought his long-standing animosities to an uncontrollable boiling point. There are strictly personal passages in this last chapter; McKay refers more than once to the fact that his intense anti-Communism has destroyed his relationships with old friends and associates in the black community. One can understand, and sympathize, with this loss of old friendships. In part, alienation was the price McKay paid for being, as noted before, ahead of his time in perceiving the insincerity of the Party's advances to the black community. His mind goes back to the "magic pilgrimage," and he expresses sympathy for the displaced aristocracy and their children that he had seen in Russia (257 - 58).

Although such a passage is a tribute to McKay's humanitarianism, the inclusion of details related to his personal grievances and to the Soviet oppression of the followers of the Czar in his essay concerning Sufi Abdul Hamid and Harlem labor tells much about the complex emotions underlying *Harlem: Negro Metropolis*. One passage toward the end of the book perhaps best illustrates the book's desperation: "The intellectual, discovered in error, is as vicious as a tiger. And in this the Negro intellectual is like any other. He fights the popular movements of his people because he knows that they are right and he is wrong" (259). One has a glimpse of the book McKay might have written when he focuses his discussion upon the necessity of black communities to develop themselves "commercially, politically, and culturally" and to produce their own "police officers, sheriffs and judges, principals of schools, landlords and businessmen" (260). Conceived at a happier time in his life, *Harlem: Negro Metropolis* might well have been an invaluable study of Harlem since the necessary insights are presented but not sufficiently and objectively developed. His long-standing faith in community solidarity does receive its most sustained analysis, however.

One remaining aspect of this final chapter merits discussion, for in it McKay's mind turns back to the 1920s and the Renaissance: "The Harlem renaissance movement of the antic nineteen twenties was really inspired and kept alive by the interest and presence of white bohemians. It faded out when they became tired of the new plaything" (248). Although men such as Van Vechten were major organizers and cheerleaders of the Renaissance, McKay's analysis ignored the vital contributions of Locke and others. To ignore them is, of course, precisely what McKay wished to do. It was his way of easing any lingering pain about the hostility with which *Home to Harlem* had been received by the black intellectual establishment approximately ten years earlier. The effect is to add to McKay's one-sidedness which plagues the entire book.

Despite the significance of *A Long Way From Home* as an account of McKay's development as a black artist and as his last aesthetically satisfying statement of black pride, and despite the moments of prophetic insight in *Harlem: Negro Metropolis*, one wishes that McKay had published fiction after *Banana Bottom.* However, as the letters to Eastman reveal, he was deeply discouraged by the failure of his Jamaican novel; and, although he did bring other manuscripts to varying stages of completion, he received no encouragement from publishers or literary agents. For instance, Wayne Cooper tells us that "Eugene Saxton, who had handled his work at Harper's, bluntly informed McKay that his popularity had been part of a passing fad."[23] Moreover, the reception of *Banana Bottom* had caused him to doubt its worth and significance. Probably a desire to produce something which the temper of the times could accept led him to autobiography and sociology. Always a highly romantic novelist, his personal suffering had made him a bitter, vindictive man; and the result is highly slanted and unsatisfactory sociology. Only in the autobiography in which he can look back to happier times does he approach the convincing power of his best fiction, and even there he strangely keeps himself hidden from his reader. Perhaps the experiences of being neglected by old friends and former readers, of working for a dollar a day in a welfare camp, and of being remembered, if at all, as an outdated symbol of a dead past made him reluctant in his autobiography to open himself more than necessary to any additional hurt. If so, one understands.

CHAPTER 6

A Long Way From Home

ONE is tempted to say of some writers that they will be remembered for their historical impact rather than for the strictly literary merit of their work. Claude McKay is such a figure: he is an uneven writer, but it is difficult to overestimate his historic importance to Afro-American and West Indian literature. *Banana Bottom* has structural flaws, and it is distinctly his best novel. He was at best a good, but not great, short-story writer; and his poetry is too often flawed by Victorian and Romantic excesses. The success of *A Long Way From Home* is of a paradoxical nature, and *Harlem: Negro Metropolis* is simply a failure. Yet, when one views the three novels as a fictional statement of black identity and when one remembers their numerous memorable passages of angry protest and of sensual impressionism, considers such excellent poems as "The Harlem Dancer," and reads *A Long Way From Home* as artistic theory centered on one individual's relationships with the philosophical and political upheavals of the twentieth century, one realizes the extent and variety of McKay's aesthetic achievement.

That achievement, in fact, makes one want more. As mentioned in Chapter 1, McKay's seeming abandonment of fiction after 1933 and the deterioration of his poetry are extremely frustrating. *A Long Way From Home* is simply not adequate compensation. The author's letters to Eastman reveal that he did not make a conscious decision to stop writing fiction after his return to the United States; he outlined several prospective novels and stories to Eastman, and Clarence Major's discovery is evidence that three projects were at least virtually completed at his death. One is the autobiographical manuscript, "My Green Hills of Jamaica," which has already been discussed. Another is an early work, "Romance in Marseilles," which McKay actually completed in 1930. Major describes it as a "thin, colorful and choppy story of a West African Black man" named

Lafala. Lafala has lost both his legs while a stowaway aboard a ship. The novel describes his attempts to sue the steamship company with the aid of a "crooked lawyer called The Black Angel." Another major character is a Marseilles prostitute named Aelima. Major writes that "thematically and even structurally 'Romance' resembles *Banjo*. . . ." McKay simply never found a publisher for "Romance in Marseilles"; and it still remains unpublished. Actually McKay had experienced comparable bad luck before. He destroyed the first novel he ever wrote entitled "Color Scheme" because its sexual frankness kept it from finding a publisher. The third manuscript examined by Major was apparently a late work. Entitled "Harlem Glory," it recounts the picaresque adventures in Harlem during the early 1930s of Buster Smith, a West Indian who "divides his time between running numbers, romancing women, and spiritualism."[1]

Throughout the last years of his life, McKay continually planned other literary projects. In a May 9, 1934, letter he was planning ". . . either a novel about Morocco or an autobiographical piece."[2] A week later, on May 15, 1934, he was on fire with both ideas: ". . . I have a *wonderful* autobiographical and a Moroccan novel to write — without any reserve." On August 12, 1934, he was still involved in both projects as well as a book of poems; but two months later he was trapped in the welfare-camp problem discussed earlier. It is not necessary to repeat his frequent complaints to Eastman that life in the camp was destructive to artistic creativity. However, while at the camp, he was preoccupied (on October 25, 1934) with still another project — a "bohemian-life book" depicting "the 1923 - 24 period" in "Berlin and Paris." Writing in November, 1934, from the camp, he told Eastman that he had ". . . an expatriate story in mind — a good one that ought to go — *if* I could write it out." That same month, he indicated that he had a finished draft of a "Marseilles novel" and that it only needed revision. By December 16, 1934, he had finished a first draft of the "expatriate story":

. . . I have a good title for it: Enigmatic Expatriate. Its [sic] about a strange little old man moving in the circle of intellectual bohemians abroad, although he is not one of them & cannot be. [sic] of his going from place to place following the bohemian caravan and his being sensitive or having a complex about the word insanity or lunacy. And he does not want to return home. I bring him along up to the time of the great bank failures, when he loses his money in one. And he decides to go home — *happy*. Then he confesses that he had been put in an assylum [sic] in America by his relatives — because of his money — He had managed to get out and go abroad where he could live eccentrically. But all the time he preferred America & now that he had no money & nothing to fear — he was happy to return at last.

One can scarcely resist the temptation to compare such a plot out-line with relevant parts of McKay's biography. Although he was also a follower of the expatriate movement, he could never really become an accepted part of it; his blackness effectively isolated him from the main body of bohemians. The character's imprisonment in an asylum under a false accusation of insanity might be regarded as a metaphor for living as a black man in white America or in the welfare camp; however, the fictional old man and McKay "preferred America" and wanted to go home. Of course, McKay's return to America was anything but happy, since he could not shed blackness as easily as the old man could his money. At any rate, McKay told Eastman in a later letter of December 19, 1934, that he liked this story better than anything he had done since *Home to Harlem*. One of course wonders what happened to it.

For a few years after his departure from the camp in late 1934 or early 1935, McKay was working on *A Long Way From Home* and *Harlem: Negro Metropolis;* but he was also contributing politically - oriented articles to several journals. In early 1941, he had turned again to fiction, and he had apparently discussed with Eastman his idea for a novel centered around leftist activities in the United States during the 1930s. His letter of March 29, 1941, concerns his progress on the novel, the extent to which he has followed Eastman's literary advice not to make it a strictly political novel, and his sense of urgency about finishing the novel. This urgency is intriguing because, since McKay was ill during most of the last fifteen years of his life, he may have feared that he would not live to complete the book. Whatever the reason for his sense of limited time, he reported a finished manuscript two months later on July 28,1941. (If this is "Harlem Glory," he certainly did follow Eastman's advice about not making it strictly political.) The novel is not mentioned again in the Eastman correspondence. For the next few years, McKay's growing interest in Catholicism dominates his letters to his old editor. As late as 1946, he was working on another book-length project, but he did not feel physically able to devote himself fully to it. Since it is described as being about his "childhood in Jamaica," one surmises that this project was "My Green Hills of Jamaica."

Possible answers to the question of what happened to such vir-tually complete (if one believes McKay's letters) works of fiction as

"Enigmatic Expatriate" and the 1930s novel is that they failed to find publishers or that their author did not even receive sufficient encouragement to complete them. McKay did not turn his back on fiction after 1933; for some reason or reasons, he simply was not able to publish any. One assumes he did not ever seriously consider a novel about Jake's life during the Depression. As stated earlier, that he did not is regrettable. Ironically, in a letter of November 10,1934, he proposed to Eastman that they attempt to get *Home to Harlem* reissued by the Modern Library.

The question of what diminished McKay's poetic output between 1934 and 1948 is easier to answer. Desperately in need of money, he felt compelled to produce either a successful novel or saleable non-fiction. He did write some poetry, however, for his conversion to Catholicism resulted in some undistinguished religious verse. More importantly, the previously discussed "Look Within" is evidence that he did return to the angry protest that had dominated his best poetry in the 1920s. On September 3, 1943, he very ambiguously informed Eastman that he was writing poetry again but that it was ". . . very different from my earlier stuff." This comment is perhaps clarified by a letter of November 28,1944, in which McKay complains that a volume of poetry has been rejected twice. In his description of the second rejection letter, he tells Eastman that the editor had said that the poems were too critical of everything and that they were "not poetry." With justifiable anger, McKay elaborates: ". . . and so, I have a hunch that I do have something that might make America feel less smug about its fascist-oppressed Negroes, while we are fighting Fascism abroad !"

Because of this statement, one assumes then that the rejected poems were comparable to "Look Within." If one accepts McKay's description of these poems, he is also inclined to believe the implication of McKay's remark that they were rejected because of their radical content; for, although the content of this volume must have again been ahead of its time, to publish poetry that is critical of a nation's foreign and domestic policy while it is fighting a war is virtually impossible. This argument does not imply that the poetry rejected in 1944 was aesthetically equal to that published during the 1920s; for it most likely was not, since "Look Within" is not a successful poem. Nevertheless, if McKay's anger was being directed at essentially the old targets of racism, injustice, and imperialism, vestiges of the power of "If We Must Die" and "The White House" might have been found in this late poetry.

McKay's description, then, of this verse as "very different from my earlier stuff" is confusing. However, the confusion is somewhat clarified in his letter of March 21, 1945, to Eastman: "Oh, I wish I had the old style! But today, I feel more like Pope and Swift or even Catullus than like Shelley and Keats and the Elizabethans." He apparently felt unable, in the mid-1940s, to be the lyric poet he had sometimes been during the peak of his career. Although the times were decidedly wrong for lyricism, one is still bothered by the implication that nature and love lyrics constituted the most significant part of his poetic achievement during the 1920s. It was, after all, "If We Must Die" that made him famous; and his reputation during the peak of his career was that of an angry black poet. Lyric poetry was a significant part of his achievement, but it had never been the most important part.

One senses a feeling in McKay that the tragedy into which the twentieth century had developed by 1945 ruled out more than simple lyricism. Seemingly, he believed that relatively indirect protest as typified by "The Harlem Dancer" was no longer viable for the black writer. Racism, American domestic injustice and international hypocrisy, and British imperialism had to be attacked directly and bluntly; undisguised satire had to supersede symbolism. It is artistically regrettable if, as seems obvious, McKay felt this necessity for pure message; but his reaction is, nevertheless, understandable.

Eastman apparently had some misgivings about the McKay poetry of this period. For one thing, he was bothered a great deal by the Jamaican's contention that America and England were morally no better than Nazi Germany. McKay defends this thesis in the Eastman letters written between 1940 and 1945 approximately as often as he defends his conversion to Catholicism. A McKay letter of September 28, 1945, leads one to believe that Eastman also had some aesthetic reservations and that, after at least two rejections, McKay had sent his poetry to his former editor for a thorough evaluation. The September 28, 1945, letter is concerned in part with McKay's reaction to this evaluation: "Yes, I like your comment and suggestion for the poems. I have taken 99% of your advice, which has cut down the lot to just a little sheaf. But I don't want to publish bad poems. I wish that those about the Communists were only a little better."

"Those about the Communists" were undoubtedly attacks upon the Party; for, by 1945, McKay was thoroughly disillusioned with Communism. It seems evident, then, that acting upon Eastman's advice, he rejected a large part of his 1940s poetic output. Even given the strong likelihood that Eastman's advice was sound, one still regrets that McKay's poetry never appeared in print.

In summary, then, McKay continued to write poetry, as he did prose in the years after his return to America; however, the political climate of the times, combined with his own mental and physical suffering, drastically reduced his poetic publication. The fact that he did continue to work in both poetry and fiction with so little tangible result emphasizes the tragedy of his life. Largely because of factors outside his control, his reputation must rest upon the works he produced between 1919 and 1937. But one should not minimize the accomplishments of those two decades.

When discussing McKay, one is tempted to fall into a fallacy comparable to that which has plagued much Scott Fitzgerald criticism — the obvious temptation to write about what both men might have done, rather than what they did. Perhaps McKay offers even more tragic possibilities for this kind of criticism than Fitzgerald, for the "waste" was much less McKay's own fault than Fitzgerald's. The author of *Home to Harlem* can be seen as a classic case of a black writer's being destroyed by the impossible pressures of his situation. He wrote a book during a period in which some Negroes were an intellectual "fad" and became famous. At a less fortuitous time, he wrote a better book which "failed." He continued to write during the worst of times for black writers and had difficulty in even getting published. One of his poems signaled the emergence of "the New Negro" in America; and, for the rest of his career, he attempted to reconcile black militancy with a personal concept of poetry which was heavily influenced by traditional concepts of form. He wished to be both a voice of black political and social ideas, and a lyric poet. Finally, he attempted to publish verse proclaiming the hypocrisy of the United States' fighting a war against Hitler while remaining a racist nation. Still, this "tragic failure" approach is as wrong for McKay as for Fitzgerald. What is finally important is that both men did produce a significant body of lasting work.

As the 1940s progressed, McKay's letters concerning ultimate racial justice in America became increasingly hopeless. In a letter of August 28, 1946, he asserted to Eastman that he did not want ". . . to go sour on humanity even after living in this awful land of the U. S. A." It is not surprising, then, that "Boyhood in Jamaica's" emphasis is upon an international black movement. There is a special irony in finding the man who had seemed to personify the concept of the American "New Negro" in 1919 advocating a new international black movement almost thirty years later, but one should not be too surprised by this fact. From the beginning, McKay was aware of the philosophical limitations of the 1920s Renaissance. From the beginning, he was searching for an aesthetic and philosophical principle based upon the concept of a unique black identity; he was never going to be limited to the boundaries of the United States in his quest for such a principle, for he did not regard himself as primarily an American or as a Jamaican, but as a black man. In *A Long Way From Home*, he stressed the importance of such a racial identity to everything he wrote, even to the poetry which does not seem to be overtly black in form or content. Moreover, despite the painful evidence of his own life, he did not finally forfeit his faith that a new, and a better, world was coming for the black man. The last two sentences of "Boyhood in Jamaica" emphasize that faith: "Happily, as I move on, I see that adventure [of the black man in white society] changing for those who will come after me. For this is the century of the coloured world."[3]

Notes and References

Chapter One

1. *Selected Poems* (New York, 1953), p. 36.
2. Saunders Redding, *To Make a Poet Black* (Chapel Hill, 1939), p. 101.
3. *A Long Way From Home* (New York, 1937), p.313.
4. Claude McKay to Max Eastman, June 28, 1933, Lilly Library, Indiana University, Bloomington, Indiana.
5. Nathan Irvin Huggins, *Harlem Renaissance* (New York,1971), p. 5.
6. Ibid., pp. 64 - 65.
7. "A Negro to his Critics," *New York Herald Tribune Books*, March 6, 1932, p. 1.
8. James Baldwin, *Notes of a Native Son* (Boston, 1955), p. 140.
9. McKay to Eastman, October 25, 1934; published in *The Passion of Claude McKay*, ed. Wayne Cooper (New York, 1973), p. 203.
10. Melvin B. Tolson, "Claude McKay's Art," *Poetry* 83 (February, 1954), 288 - 89.
11. Kenneth Ramchand, *The West Indian Novel and its Background* (New York, 1970), pp. 14 - 15.
12. McKay to Eastman, December 3, 1934; published in *The Passion of Claude McKay*, p. 211.
13. "Boyhood in Jamaica," *Phylon* 14 (1953), 134.
14. Ibid., p. 145.
15. Clarence Major, "Dear Jake and Ray," *American Poetry Review* 4 (1975), 40 - 42.
16. McKay to Eastman, June 30, 1944, Lilly Library.
17. "Speech to the Fourth Congress of The Third Communist International, Moscow," in *The Passion of Claude McKay*, pp. 91 - 95.
18. "How Black Sees Green and Red," *Liberator* 4 (June, 1921), 17.
19. Ibid., p. 20.
20. Stephen H. Bronz, *Roots of Negro Racial Consciousness* (New York, 1964), pp. 76 - 77.
21. McKay to Eastman, June 1, 1944, Lilly Library.

22. McKay to Eastman, June 30, 1944, Lilly Library.

23. Ibid.

24. Ibid.

25. "On Becoming a Roman Catholic," *The Epistle* 2 (Spring, 1945), 43 - 45.

26. McKay to Eastman, June 30, 1944, Lilly Library.

27. McKay to Eastman, October 16, 1944; published in *The Passion of Claude McKay*, p. 305.

28. "On Becoming a Roman Catholic," 43.

Chapter Two

1. *A Long Way From Home* (New York, 1937), p. 31.

2. McKay to Eastman, March 23, 1939, Lilly Library.

3. Huggins, *Harlem Renaissance*, p. 72.

4. Ibid.

5. Ibid., p. 151.

6. *Selected Poems* (New York, 1953), p. 61; subsequent references to this volume are by page in the text.

7. "Author's Word," *Harlem Shadows* (New York, 1922).

8. *Long Way From Home*, p. 314.

9. Ibid.

10. Ibid., p. 313.

11. Eugenia W. Collier sees the poem as illustrating McKay's "double consciousness": his ability to combine a positive sense of self with a realization of white society's negative view of him as a Negro. "The Four-Way Dilemma of Claude McKay," *College Language Association Journal* 15 (March, 1972), 349 - 50.

12. Melvin B. Tolson, "Claude McKay's Art," *Poetry* 83 (February, 1954), 288 - 89.

13. Ibid., 289.

14. Ibid.

Chapter Three

1. W. E. B. DuBois, "The Browsing Reader," *The Crisis* 35 (June, 1928), 202.

2. Huggins, *Harlem Renaissance*, p. 115.

3. For an excellent discussion of the factors behind the hostile receptions of *Home to Harlem* and *Banjo* by black critics, see Stephen H. Bronz, *Roots of Negro Racial Consciousness* (New York, 1964), pp. 84 - 85.

4. Huggins, *Harlem Renaissance*, p. 126.

5. David Littlejohn, *Black on White* (New York, 1966), p. 50.

6. Ibid., p. 57.

7. Bronz, *Roots of Negro Racial Consciousness*, p. 80.

8. *A Long Way From Home* (New York, 1937), p. 110.

9. Ibid., p. 4.

10. George E. Kent, "The Soulful Way of Claude McKay," *Black World* 20 (November, 1970), 37.

11. For instance, Jacqueline Kaye, "Claude McKay's 'Banjo,' " *Présence Africaine* 73 (1970), 165 - 69.

12. *Home to Harlem* (New York, 1928), p.15; subsequent references to this work are by page in the text.

13. *Banjo* (New York, 1929), p. 130; subsequent references to this work are by page in the text.

14. *A Long Way From Home*, p. 250.

15. Ibid.

16. Ibid., p. 252.

17. Ibid., p. 250.

18. Robert A. Bone, *The Negro Novel in America*, rev. ed. (New Haven, 1965), p. 69.

19. Ibid., p. 69.

20. Huggins, *Harlem Renaissance*, p. 125.

21. Ibid.

22. Richard K. Barksdale, "Symbolism and Irony in McKay's *Home to Harlem*," *College Language Association Journal* 15 (March, 1972), 338 - 44.

23. Littlejohn, *Black on White*, p. 57.

24. Huggins, *Harlem Renaissance*, p. 123.

25. Kaye, "Claude McKay's 'Banjo,' " 165.

26. Kent,"Soulful Way of Claude McKay," 41.

27. Bone, *Negro Novel in America*, p. 70.

28. Ibid., p. 72.

29. Bronz, *Roots of Negro Racial Consciousness*, p. 86.

30. Ramchand, *West Indian Novel and its Background*, p. 261.

31. *Banana Bottom* (New York, 1933), p. 84; subsequent references to this work are by page in the text.

32. Bone, *Negro Novel in America*, p. 72.

33. Kent, "Soulful Way of Claude McKay," 49.

34. Ramchand, *West Indian Novel and its Background*, p. 262.

Chapter Four

1. *Gingertown* (New York, 1932), p. 247; subsequent references to this collection are by page in the text.

2. *A Long Way From Home*, (New York, 1937), p. 247.

Chapter Five

1. Rebecca Chalmers Barton,"*A Long Way From Home*: Claude McKay," in *Witnesses for Freedom: Negro Americans in Autobiography* (New York, 1948), p. 136.

2. Ibid., p. 135.

3. Ibid., pp. 145 - 46.

4. Ibid., p. 144.

5. *A Long Way From Home* (New York, 1937), p. 4; subsequent references to this work are by page in the text.

6. Wayne Cooper, introduction to *The Passion of Claude McKay* (New York, 1973), pp. 7 - 8.

7. Wayne Cooper and Robert C. Reinders, "A Black Briton Comes 'Home': Claude McKay in England, 1920," *Race* 9, no. 1 (July, 1967), published for the Institute of Race Relations, London, by the Oxford University Press, pp. 67 - 83.

8. Ibid., p. 78.

9. McKay to Eastman, May, 1925, Lilly Library.

10. Cooper and Reinders, "Black Briton Comes 'Home,' " p. 80.

11. Ibid., pp. 73 - 74.

12. McKay to Eastman, May 18, 1923; published in *The Passion of Claude McKay*.

13. Cooper and Reinders, "Black Briton Comes 'Home,' " p. 80.

14. Bronz, *Roots of Negro Racial Consciousness*, pp. 78 - 79.

15. McKay to Eastman, May, 1925, Lilly Library.

16. Ibid.

17. McKay to Eastman, March 2, 1939, Lilly Library.

18. "Harlem Runs Wild," *The Nation* 140 (April 3, 1935), 383.

19. Ibid., 382.

20. Ibid., 383.

21. *Harlem: Negro Metropolis* (New York, 1940), p. 15; subsequent references to this work are by page in the text.

22. For a good discussion of the conflict between Garvey and black leaders such as DuBois and A. Philip Randolph, see Huggins, *Harlem Renaissance*, pp. 43 - 45.

23. Cooper, introduction to *Passion of Claude McKay*, p. 36.

Chapter Six

1. Major, "Dear Jake and Ray," *American Poetry Review* 4 (1975), 40 - 42.

2. McKay to Eastman, May 9, 1934; published in *The Passion of Claude McKay*. Since virtually all citations in this chapter are to letters from McKay to Eastman, subsequent references to such letters are by date in the text.

3. "Boyhood in Jamaica," *Phylon* 14 (1953), 145.

Selected Bibliography

PRIMARY SOURCES

1. Books

Banana Bottom. New York: Harper, 1933; reprint, Chatham, New Jersey: Chatham Bookseller, 1970.

Banjo. New York: Harper, 1929; paperback reprint, New York: Harcourt Brace Jovanovich, n.d.

Constab Ballads. London: Watts, 1912. Contains a preface by McKay.

The Dialect Poetry of Claude McKay. Freeport, New York: Books for Libraries Press, 1972. Reprints *Songs of Jamaica* and *Constab Ballads* with a new introduction by Wayne Cooper.

Gingertown. New York: Harper, 1932.

Harlem: Negro Metropolis. New York: E. P. Dutton, 1940; paperback reprint, New York: Harcourt Brace Jovanovich, n.d.

Harlem Shadows. Introductions by Max Eastman and McKay. New York: Harcourt Brace, 1922.

Home to Harlem. New York: Harper, 1928; paperback reprint, New York: Pocket Books, 1965.

A Long Way From Home. New York: Furman, 1937; paperback reprint, New York: Harcourt Brace, 1970. Introduction by St. Clair Drake.

The Passion of Claude McKay: Selected Prose and Poetry, 1912 - 1948. Edited by Wayne Cooper. New York: Schocken Books, 1973.

Selected Poems of Claude McKay. Introduction by John Dewey and a biographical sketch by Max Eastman. New York: Bookman Associates, 1953; paperback reprint containing biographical sketch by Eastman, New York: Harcourt Brace, n.d.

Songs of Jamaica. Preface by Walter Jekyll. London: Gardner, 1912; reprint, Miami, Florida: Mnemosyne, 1969.

Spring in New Hampshire and Other Poems. Introduction by I. A. Richards. London: Richards, 1920.

2. Uncollected Published Pieces

"Boyhood in Jamaica,"*Phylon* 14 (1953), 134 - 45; essay.

"Harlem Runs Wild," *The Nation* 140 (April 3, 1935), 382 - 83; essay.
"He Who Gets Slapped," *Liberator* 5 (May, 1922), 24 - 25; essay.
"How Black Sees Green and Red," *Liberator* 4 (June, 1921), 17 - 21; essay.
"Lest We Forget," *Jewish Frontier* 7 (January, 1940), 9 - 11; essay.
"The Middle Ages," *Catholic Worker* 13 (May, 1946), 5; poem.
"A Negro to his Critics," *New York Herald Tribune Books*, March 6, 1932,
    pp. 1, 6; essay.
"The New Day," *Interracial Review* 19 (March, 1946), 37; poem.
"On Becoming a Roman Catholic," *The Epistle* 2 (Spring, 1945), 43 - 45; es-
    say.
"Why I Became a Catholic," *Ebony* 1 (March, 1946), 32; essay.

3. Anthologized Collections
Four Negro Poets. Edited by Alain Locke. New York: Simon and Schuster,
    1927. Contains an introduction by Locke, ten poems by McKay, and
    poetry by Jean Toomer, Countee Cullen, and Langston Hughes.

4. Unpublished Correspondence
McKay's unpublished letters to Max Eastman are in the Lilly Library, In-
    diana University, Bloomington, Indiana.

SECONDARY SOURCES

1. Books
BARTON, REBECCA CHALMERS. *Witnesses for Freedom: Negro Americans in
    Autobiography.* New York: Harper, 1948. Chapter entitled "A Long
    Way From Home: Claude McKay" treats McKay's autobiography
    primarily as a statement of individualism.
BONE, ROBERT A. *The Negro Novel in America.* New Haven: Yale, 1958;
    revised edition, 1965. Underrates *Home to Harlem*; still one of the
    most significant discussions of thematic progression in McKay's
    novels.
BRONZ, STEPHEN H. *Roots of Negro Racial Consciousness.* New York: Libra,
    1964. Generally sympathetic discussion of McKay's writing; most
    valuable for information concerning the Renaissance and McKay's
    life.
GAYLE, ADDISON, JR. *The Way of the New World: The Black Novel in
    America.* New York: Anchor Press, 1975. Contains sound discussion of
    McKay's three published novels as revolving around the search for a
    lost black identity. Argues that *Banana Bottom* is the best novel.
GLOSTER, HUGH M. *Negro Voices in American Fiction.* Chapel Hill, North
    Carolina: University of North Carolina Press, 1948. Conservative
    study; largely unsympathetic to McKay's fiction.
HUGGINS, NATHAN IRVIN. *Harlem Renaissance.* New York: Oxford University
    Press, 1971. Valuable for its analysis of the promise and the actuality

of the Renaissance and for its discussion of McKay's commitment to formal style and diction in poetry.

LITTLEJOHN, DAVID. *Black on White*. New York: Grossman, 1966. Shallow and hostile discussion of McKay.

RAMCHAND, KENNETH. *The West Indian Novel and its Background*. New York: Barnes and Noble, 1970. Sees McKay as the forerunner of West Indian fiction; valuable, intelligent analysis of McKay's novels.

REDDING, SAUNDERS. *To Make a Poet Black*. Chapel Hill, North Carolina: University of North Carolina Press, 1939. Sympathetic analysis of McKay's poetry.

ROSENBLATT, ROGER. *Black Fiction*. Cambridge, Massachusetts: Harvard University Press, 1974. Contains a shallow discussion of *Home to Harlem* as an unstructured exercise in "primitivism."

2. Essays

BARKSDALE, RICHARD K. "Symbolism and Irony in McKay's *Home to Harlem*," *College Language Association Journal* 15 (March, 1972), 338 - 44. Treats structure of *Home* as more than episodic and disjointed.

BUTCHER, PHILIP. "If We Must Die," *Opportunity* 26 (1948), 127. Evaluation of McKay upon his death.

CARTEY, WILFRED. "Five Shadows of Harlem," *Negro Digest* 18 (August, 1969), 22 - 25, 83 - 92. Comparison of the treatment of Harlem in poetry by McKay, Federico Garcia Lorca, Leopold Sedor Senghor, and Langston Hughes.

COLLIER, EUGENIA W. "The Four-Way Dilemma of Claude McKay," *College Language Association Journal* 15 (March, 1972), 345 - 53. Interesting outline of main contradictions inherent in McKay's life and writing.

CONROY, SISTER MARY. "The Vagabond Motif in the Writings of Claude McKay," *Negro American Literature Forum* 5 (Spring, 1971), 15 - 23. Especially valuable for its discussion of *Gingertown*.

COOPER, WAYNE, and REINDERS, ROBERT C., "A Black Briton Comes Home: Claude McKay in England," *Race* 9 (1967), 67 - 83. Invaluable for information concerning McKay's English sojourn and his association with Sylvia Pankhurst's *Workers' Dreadnought*.

COOPER, WAYNE. "Claude McKay and the New Negro of the 1920's," *Phylon* 25 (1964), 297 - 306. Valuable treatment of McKay's relationship to the Harlem Renaissance.

DUBOIS, W. E. B. "The Browsing Reader," *The Crisis* 35 (June, 1928), 202. Famous hostile review of *Home to Harlem*.

JACKSON, BLYDEN. "The Essential McKay," *Phylon* 14 (1953), 216 - 17. Largely sympathetic review of *The Selected Poems* of McKay.

KAYE, JACQUELINE. "Claude McKay's 'Banjo,'" *Présence Africaine* 73 (1970), 165 - 69. Important analysis of *Banjo*'s contribution to the concept of Negritude.

KENT, GEORGE E. "The Soulful Way of Claude McKay," *Black World* 20 (November, 1970), 37 - 51. Easily the best article yet published about McKay's fiction; focuses upon his black consciousness.

LARSON, CHARLES R. "Three Harlem Novels of the Jazz Age," *Critique* 11 (1969), 66 - 78. Treats *Home to Harlem* in a generally unsympathetic manner.

MAJOR, CLARENCE. "Dear Jake and Ray," *American Poetry Review* 4 (1975), 40 - 42. Invaluable discussion of the three unpublished McKay manuscripts, "My Green Hills of Jamaica," "Romance in Marseilles," and "Harlem Glory."

SMITH, ROBERT A. "Claude McKay: An Essay in Criticism," *Phylon* 9 (1948), 270 - 73. Evaluation of McKay upon his death.

TOLSON, MELVIN B. "Claude McKay's Art," *Poetry* 83 (February, 1954), 287 - 90. Review of McKay's *Selected Poems*; provides perhaps the most intelligent discussion yet published of the conservative form and "revolutionary content" of McKay's poetry.

Index